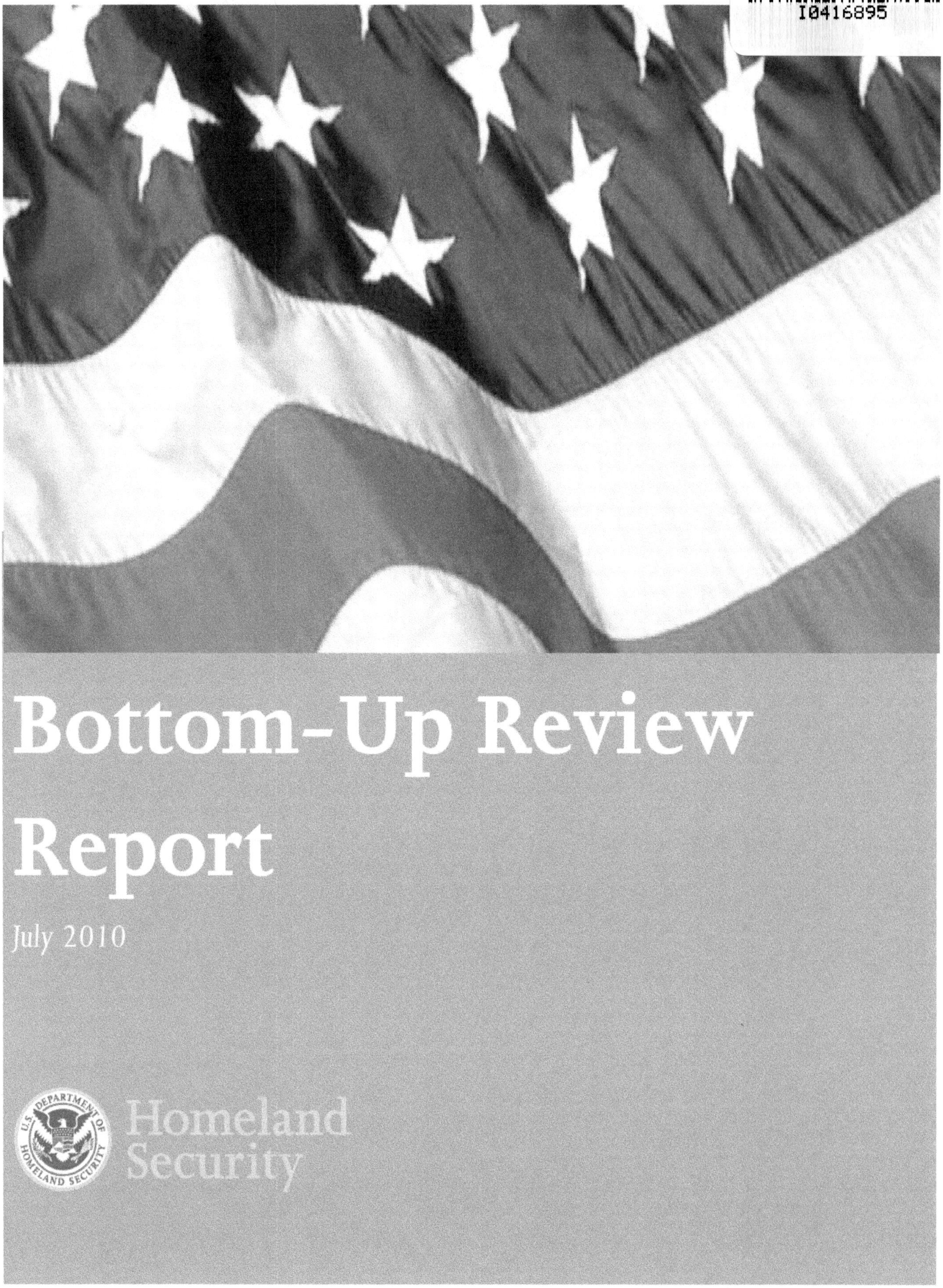

Bottom-Up Review Report

July 2010

Homeland
Security

Table of Contents

Secretary

U.S. Department of Homeland Security
Washington, DC 20528

In February 2010, the Department of Homeland Security published our Nation's first ever comprehensive review of America's strategy for homeland security—the Quadrennial Homeland Security Review (QHSR). The QHSR was the first step in setting forth the strategic path forward to guide the activities of the homeland security enterprise toward a common end: a homeland that is safe, secure, and resilient against terrorism and other hazards where American interests, aspirations, and way of life can thrive. The QHSR accomplished this by laying out a vision for a secure homeland, key mission priorities, and specific goals for each of those mission areas. The QHSR is consistent with, and expands upon, the recently-released *National Security Strategy*.

At the same time, the QHSR and the bottom-up review (BUR) processes reflect the enormity of the ongoing challenge of building OneDHS from previously separate organizations and entities. The QHSR and BUR processes intentionally challenge us to consider difficult questions regarding the mission, organization, and priorities of homeland security. Forging a single integrated and optimized Department out of components extracted from previously fully-formed and functioning agencies has been a great challenge for every leadership team at DHS since its founding.

The QHSR identified five core mission areas of homeland security—preventing terrorism and enhancing security, securing and managing our borders, enforcing and administering our immigration laws, safeguarding and securing cyberspace, and ensuring resilience to disasters. These missions, and the associated goals defined in the QHSR, comprise the backbone of what it takes to keep America safe, secure, and resilient. The QHSR was a first and essential step of a multi-step process to answer key questions regarding what must be done to accomplish the missions of homeland security. The underlying premise of the BUR was the need to also examine programs, plans, structures, and resources from the bottom up.

The BUR provides the results of an unprecedented Department-wide assessment of DHS, begun in November 2009, to align the Department's programmatic activities and organizational structure with the mission sets and goals identified in the QHSR. The BUR report focuses on the following questions:

- How can we strengthen the Department's performance in each of the five mission areas?

- How should we improve Departmental operations and management?

- How can we increase accountability for the resources entrusted to DHS?

The BUR will serve as a road map for these questions. First and foremost, it provides direction for reinforcing the cornerstone of homeland security: preventing terrorism. The BUR also focuses on combating cybersecurity threats, ensuring resilience to all hazards, and the critical need to reform our immigration system. It also provides new emphasis on the importance of enhancing the security and resilience of the global systems that are responsible for the movement of people and goods across our borders. Finally, the review lays a foundation for improving Departmental operations and management and increasing accountability for the resources entrusted to DHS.

I am very proud of the work done every day by the men and women in the Department of Homeland Security as well as the hundreds of thousands of Federal, State, local, tribal, and territorial officials, private citizens, and businesses with whom we partner to keep America safe, secure, and resilient. We have accomplished much and have much more to accomplish together in the years ahead. The QHSR and the results of the BUR in this report will guide these important efforts.

Secretary Janet Napolitano

Preface

In 2007, the Homeland Security Act of 2002 was amended to require the Department of Homeland Security (DHS) to initiate implementation of a Quadrennial Homeland Security Reviews (QHSR) in 2009, and to conduct subsequent reviews every four years thereafter. The purpose of the QHSR was to describe the threats to the national security interests of the Nation, outline and prioritize the full range of homeland security missions, and update the national homeland security strategy. It would also assess the alignment of the Department to the strategy, promote mechanisms for turning strategic requirements into an acquisition strategy and expenditure plan, and identify the budget plan for successfully executing the homeland security missions.

DHS conducted the first QHSR in 2009, and delivered the QHSR Report to Congress on February 1, 2010. The QHSR was a comprehensive examination of the homeland security strategy of the Nation and included recommendations regarding the long-term strategy and priorities of the Nation for homeland security. The QHSR Report included the results of the QHSR, a national homeland security strategy, a description of the critical homeland security missions of the Nation, and an explanation of the underlying assumptions used in conducting the review. The QHSR is consistent with, and expands upon, the recently-released *National Security Strategy*.

A bottom-up review (BUR) of the Department of Homeland Security was initiated in November 2009 as an immediate follow-on and complement to the QHSR. The BUR included an assessment of the organizational alignment of the Department with the homeland security missions set forth in the QHSR, including the Department's organizational structure, management systems, procurement systems, and physical and technical infrastructure. The BUR also included a review and assessment of the effectiveness of the mechanisms of the Department for turning the requirements developed in the QHSR into an acquisition strategy and expenditure plan within the Department.

The BUR resulted in a comprehensive catalogue of DHS activities across the homeland security missions, as well as a list of over 300 potential initiatives and enhancements. The BUR Report distills the results of this analysis, describing the alignment of the Department with the homeland security missions, and setting forth the Department's priority initiatives and enhancements to increase mission performance, improve Departmental management, and increase accountability over the next four years. The BUR Report includes recommendations for improving the organizational alignment of the Department and enhancing its business processes.

The BUR is the second step of a three-step process. The Department's FY 2012 budget request will begin the process of implementing the BUR initiatives and enhancements, and the corresponding FY 2012-2016 Future Years Homeland Security Program will set forth the budget plan required to provide sufficient resources to successfully execute the Department's responsibilities across the full range of homeland security missions as described in the QHSR, with a priority placed on the initiatives and enhancements set forth in the BUR Report. As such, the BUR Report is not a budget request and does not describe specific budget requests for FY 2012 or for subsequent years. Nor is the BUR Report a strategic plan. Consequently, it neither includes performance measures nor attaches resources to strategic goals and objectives, nor does it describe the sequence in which DHS will seek to implement the initiatives and enhancements described herein. Instead, the BUR Report sets forth DHS's conclusions concerning the priority initiatives and enhancements necessary to strengthen existing programs and address priority capability and capacity gaps over the FY 2012-2016 period, in order to set a foundation for future success.

Executive Summary

The Department of Homeland Security (DHS) was formed in the wake of the terrorist attacks of September 11, 2001, as part of a deliberate and determined national effort to safeguard the United States against terrorism. DHS became the third-largest Federal department, bringing together 22 different Federal agencies, each with a role in this effort. Integrating these many disparate entities—some with long histories of independent or autonomous operations, and all with distinct operational cultures—while maintaining their unique strengths and capabilities has presented significant public policy and management challenges.

The submission of the Quadrennial Homeland Security Review (QHSR) Report to Congress on February 1, 2010 marked an important first step in a multi-step process to examine and address fundamental issues that concern homeland security. The QHSR Report described the Nation's homeland security interests, identified the critical homeland security missions, and defined a strategic approach to those missions by laying out the principal goals, essential objectives, and key strategic outcomes necessary for that approach to succeed. A bottom-up review (BUR) of the Department of Homeland Security was initiated in November 2009 as an immediate follow-on and complement to the congressionally mandated QHSR with the aim to align the Department's programmatic activities and organizational structure with the broader mission sets and goal identified in the QHSR. This report reflects that endeavor and represents an intermediate step between the QHSR Report and the DHS FY 2012-2016 Future Years Homeland Security Program (FYHSP), which will propose specific programmatic adjustments based on the QHSR strategic framework. Together, these three elements—the QHSR, the BUR, and the DHS FY 2012-2016 FYHSP—will address the primary legislative requirements set forth in Section 707 of the Homeland Security Act.

The aims of the BUR were several-fold: first, to gauge how well current activities and departmental organization align with mission priorities and goals as outlined in the QHSR; second, to identify ways to achieve better programmatic and budgetary alignment across the entire department; third, to identify areas for enhanced mission performance; and fourth, to prioritize initiatives to strengthen existing programs and organization, address shortfalls, and establish a foundation for innovation and advancement. DHS conducted extensive analysis of its current activities and organization in light of the mission goals and objectives set forth in the QHSR Report. The BUR Report describes DHS's current activities within each of the homeland security missions based on current authorities and roles and responsibilities, and sets forth DHS's conclusions concerning the priority initiatives and enhancements necessary to strengthen existing programs, address shortfalls, and set a foundation for future success.

While the robust portfolio of DHS's component agencies cannot be completely represented, this report briefly discusses the Department's core role in each of the homeland security missions, considers the additional statutory responsibilities of DHS component agencies, and outlines enhancements and initiatives that address three principal areas of emphasis:

- Strengthen and Mature DHS—There is a need to strengthen the Department's ability to execute its mission responsibilities, run itself, and account for the resources that have been entrusted to it.

- Enhance Partner Capability and Capacity—Responsibilities for homeland security are broader than those of DHS and indeed broader than those of the Federal government. For that reason, there is a need to strengthen the ability of partners in the homeland security enterprise—in particular, State, local, tribal, and territorial governments, and the private sector—to execute important aspects of core homeland security mission activities.

- Deepen International Engagement—Security of our homeland begins far from our shores. We must work with key international partners to improve the critical partnerships and activities that affect the homeland security mission space, consistent with the broad range of U.S. Government international priorities and in consultation and coordination with the Department of State and the U.S. Chiefs of Mission stationed in foreign countries.

DHS used three criteria to evaluate initiatives and identify enhancements:

- Does the initiative offer the opportunity to advance the safety, security, and resilience of the homeland beyond incremental improvements to current activities?

- Is the initiative sufficiently defined to permit the identification of performance objectives, measures, and targets?

- Can the initiative be achieved within the FY 2012-2016 timeframe?

Mission 1: Preventing Terrorism and Enhancing Security

Protecting the United States and its people from terrorism is the cornerstone of homeland security. DHS shares leadership roles and responsibilities in the U.S. government's efforts to prevent terrorist attacks with several Federal departments and agencies. DHS's responsibilities focus on three goals: preventing terrorist attacks; preventing the unauthorized acquisition, importation, movement, or use of chemical, biological, radiological, and nuclear (CBRN) materials and capabilities within the United States; and reducing the vulnerability of critical infrastructure, key leadership, and events to terrorist attacks and other hazards. To improve performance in this mission area, the Department will:

- Strengthen counterterrorism coordination across DHS;

- Strengthen aviation security by bolstering the international aviation security system, improving security processes and technologies, and encouraging partnerships with industry;

- Create an integrated Departmental information sharing architecture and link that architecture to interagency efforts to prevent terrorism while protecting privacy, civil rights and civil liberties;

- Deliver infrastructure protection and resilience capabilities to the field, in conjunction with efforts to "design in" greater resilience in critical infrastructure;

- Set national performance standards for identification verification;

- Increase efforts to detect and counter nuclear and biological weapons and dangerous materials;

- Standardize and institutionalize the National Fusion Center Network;

- Promote safeguards for access to secure areas in critical facilities, including through increased risk-informed screening and recurrent vetting;

- Establish DHS as a center for excellence for canine training and deployment; and

- Redesign the Federal Protective Service to better match mission requirements.

Mission 2: Securing and Managing Our Borders

We are responsible for secure, well-managed borders that not only protect the United States against threats from abroad, but also expedite the safe flow of lawful travel and commerce. Achieving this outcome rests on three interrelated goals: effectively securing U.S. air, land, and sea borders; safeguarding lawful trade and travel; and disrupting and dismantling transnational criminal and terrorist organizations. To strengthen efforts to achieve these goals, the Department will:

- Expand joint operations and intelligence capabilities, including enhanced domain awareness;

- Enhance the security of the global trade and travel systems responsible for the secure movement of people and goods, including enhanced container and maritime security and prioritization of immigration and customs investigations relating to global trade and travel systems;

- Strengthen and expand DHS-related security assistance internationally (e.g. border integrity and customs enforcement security assistance) consistent with U.S. government security and foreign assistance objectives in consultation and coordination with the Departments of State and Defense; and

- Work closely with the governments of Canada and Mexico to enhance North American security.

Mission 3: Enforcing and Administering Our Immigration Laws

Smart and effective enforcement and administration of our immigration laws allows the government to facilitate lawful immigration while identifying and removing those who violate our laws. To support this mission area, DHS will:

- Pursue comprehensive immigration reform;

- Strengthen and improve the Department's immigration services process;

- Prioritize national security and fraud detection vetting in immigration services processes;

- Target egregious employers who knowingly exploit illegal workers;

- Dismantle human smuggling organizations through concerted law enforcement activity;

- Improve the detention and removal process by increasing non-investigatory law enforcement staffing and expanding Secure Communities and the Criminal Alien Program;

- Work with new Americans so that they fully transition to the rights and responsibilities of citizenship; and

- Build and maintain a model immigration detention system.

Mission 4: Safeguarding and Securing Cyberspace

Cyber infrastructure forms the backbone of the Nation's economy and connects every aspect of our way of life. While the cyber environment offers the potential for rapid technological advancement and economic growth, a range of malicious actors may seek to exploit cyberspace for dangerous or harmful purposes, disrupt communications or other services, and attack the Nation's infrastructure through cyber means. By statute and Presidential directive, DHS has the lead for the Federal government to secure civilian government computer systems, works with industry to defend privately-owned and operated critical infrastructure, and works with State, local, tribal and territorial governments to secure their information systems. In pursuing these initiatives and enhancements to strengthen the Department's capabilities in cybersecurity, DHS will:

- Better integrate and focus DHS cybersecurity and infrastructure resilience operations;

- Strengthen DHS ability to protect cyber networks;

- Increase predictive, investigative, and forensic capabilities for cyber intrusions and attacks; and

- Promote cybersecurity public awareness through the cyber awareness program and the planned implementation of a national public awareness and education campaign.

Mission 5: Ensuring Resilience to Disasters

Ensuring domestic resilience to disasters is grounded in the four fundamental elements of emergency management: mitigating hazards, increasing our Nation's preparedness, effectively responding to emergencies, and supporting community recovery. During domestic disasters, the Department's role, largely executed through the Federal Emergency Management Agency (FEMA), is principally one of coordinator, working closely with our State, local, regional, tribal, and territorial partners, as well as nongovernmental organizations and the private sector, to enhance preparedness, build and sustain capabilities, and act as an aggregator of resources from across the Federal government. DHS, through FEMA, also has specific direct responsibilities, including disaster response and field coordination, disaster logistics, individual and public assistance programs, as well as national continuity programs. DHS maintains a significant first responder capability for disasters in the maritime domain through the U.S. Coast Guard (USCG), and also ensures the resilience of critical infrastructure to disasters through the National Protection and Programs Directorate. In order to strengthen mission performance, DHS will:

- Enhance catastrophic disaster preparedness at the Federal, State, local, tribal, and territorial levels, as well as within nongovernmental organizations and the private sector, through nationally agreed-upon, risk-based preparedness standards;

- Improve the capabilities of DHS to lead in emergency management through a new strategic approach to developing FEMA's workforce, creating an emergency management career path, and harmonizing first responder training across DHS;

- Explore opportunities with the private sector to "design-in" greater resilience for critical infrastructure; and

- Make individual and family preparedness and critical facility resilience inherent in community preparedness.

Complementary Department Responsibilities and Hybrid Capabilities

DHS also performs a number of services and functions that are complementary to its homeland security mission responsibilities, including marine safety, stewardship, and environmental protection, and certain categories of law enforcement activities. These services and functions are typically performed with hybrid capabilities—assets and resources capable of performing multiple missions—which are a hallmark of homeland security. For example, the same assets and personnel that patrol our borders, enforce our immigration laws, and respond to major oil spills also enforce safety regulations, assist travelers, and safeguard natural resources. These complementary activities are critical to fulfilling other national interests and are often intertwined with and mutually supporting of homeland security activities.

Improving Department Management

The integration of 22 different Federal departments and agencies into a unified, integrated Department of Homeland Security continues to represent a significant public policy and management challenge. Over the course of its brief history, DHS has evolved to its current structure, which includes seven operating components, four headquarters directorates, and over 15 additional supporting offices, many of which combine responsibilities for policy, management, operations, acquisition, external affairs, and research and development. In order to improve department management, DHS proposes to:

- Seek restoration of the Secretary's reorganizational authority for DHS headquarters to address new threats and realize greater efficiencies;

- Realign component regional configurations into a single DHS regional structure;

- Improve cross-Departmental management, policy, and functional integration;

- Strengthen DHS internal counterintelligence capabilities and internal intelligence sharing and distribution;

- Enhance the Department's risk management capability;

- Invest in the DHS workforce and improve retention and morale by strengthening employee health and wellness programs;

- Strengthen coordination within DHS through cross-Departmental training and career paths;

- Increase diversity in the DHS workforce, especially at senior levels; and

- Balance the DHS workforce by ensuring strong federal control of all DHS work and reducing reliance on contractors as needed to enhance competency and meet long-term mission requirements.

Increasing Accountability

To enhance mission performance and improve Departmental management, DHS must increase accountability across the organization. While accountability cuts across all aspects of the organization's operations, our initial focus will be to maximize the performance and resource data we collect to support strategic and risk-informed decision-making. The initiatives described below are intended to improve the effectiveness of the Department in turning the requirements developed in the QHSR into an acquisition strategy and expenditure plan. DHS proposes to:

- Increase its analytic capability and capacity by enhancing strategic planning, resource allocation, risk analysis, net assessment, modeling capabilities, statistical analysis, and data collection;

- Improve performance measurement and accountability by increasing the quality of the Department's performance measures and linking those measures to the mission outcomes articulated in the QHSR Report; and

- Strengthen acquisition oversight by strengthening the Department's independent cost estimation capability.

I. Introduction

The submission of the Quadrennial Homeland Security Review (QHSR) Report to Congress on February 1, 2010 marked an important first step in a multi-step process to examine and address fundamental issues that concern homeland security. The QHSR Report described the Nation's homeland security interests, identified the critical homeland security missions, and defined a strategic approach to those missions by laying out the principal goals, essential objectives, and key strategic outcomes necessary for that strategic approach to succeed.

Figure 1. Homeland Security Missions and Goals

Mission 1: Preventing Terrorism and Enhancing Security

- Goal 1.1: Prevent Terrorist Attacks
- Goal 1.2: Prevent the Unauthorized Acquisition or Use of Chemical, Biological, Radiological, and Nuclear Materials and Capabilities
- Goal 1.3: Manage Risks to Critical Infrastructure, Key Leadership, and Events

Mission 2: Securing and Managing Our Borders

- Goal 2.1: Effectively Control U.S. Air, Land, and Sea Borders
- Goal 2.2: Safeguard Lawful Trade and Travel
- Goal 2.3: Disrupt and Dismantle Transnational Criminal Organizations

Mission 3: Enforcing and Administering Our Immigration Laws

- Goal 3.1: Strengthen and Effectively Administer the Immigration System
- Goal 3.2: Prevent Unlawful Immigration

Mission 4: Safeguarding and Securing Cyberspace

- Goal 4.1: Create a Safe, Secure, and Resilient Cyber Environment
- Goal 4.2: Promote Cybersecurity Knowledge and Innovation

Mission 5: Ensuring Resilience to Disasters

- Goal 5.1: Mitigate Hazards
- Goal 5.2: Enhance Preparedness
- Goal 5.3: Ensure Effective Emergency Response
- Goal 5.4: Rapidly Recover

This comprehensive, enterprise-wide strategic framework for homeland security provided the foundation for the next step: a deeper, bottom-up review of the Department of Homeland Security (DHS) programs and activities required to execute the homeland security missions. The bottom-up review (BUR) of DHS was initiated in November 2009 as an immediate follow-on and complement to the QHSR with the aim to align the Department's programmatic activities and organizational structure with the broader mission sets and goals identified in the QHSR.

This report is one result of that effort and represents an intermediate step between the QHSR Report and the DHS FY 2012 budget submission and corresponding FY 2012-2016 Future Years Homeland Security Program to Congress, which will propose specific programmatic adjustments based on the QHSR strategic framework. It provides the bridge between the homeland security enterprise-level discussion in the QHSR Report and DHS responsibilities as they relate not only to the homeland security missions, but also to a number of other Departmental responsibilities as executed principally through several of its key operating components.

Approach to the Bottom-Up Review

The bottom-up review process gave DHS the opportunity to review its programmatic activities and organizational structure in depth. The aims were several-fold: first, to gauge how well current activities and departmental organization aligned with mission priorities and goals as outlined in the QHSR; second, to identify ways to achieve better programmatic and budgetary alignment across the entire department; third, to identify gaps in mission execution; and fourth, to prioritize initiatives to strengthen existing programs and organization, fill key gaps, and establish a foundation for innovation and advancement.

Three questions guided our work:

- How can we strengthen the Department's mission performance?

- How should we improve Departmental operations and management?

- How can we increase accountability for the resources entrusted to DHS?

DHS conducted extensive analysis of its current activities and organization in light of the mission goals and objectives set forth in the QHSR Report. The BUR Report describes DHS's current activities within each of the homeland security missions based on current authorities and roles and responsibilities, and sets forth DHS's conclusions concerning the priority initiatives and enhancements necessary to strengthen existing programs, fill shortfalls, and set a foundation for future success.

DHS used three criteria to evaluate mission, management, and accountability initiatives and identify enhancements:

- Does the initiative offer the opportunity to advance the safety, security, and resilience of the homeland beyond incremental improvements to current activities?

- Is the initiative sufficiently defined to permit the identification of performance objectives, measures, and targets?

- Can the initiative be achieved within the FY 2012-2016 timeframe?

In identifying initiatives across the homeland security mission space, three principal areas of emphasis became clear:

- Strengthen and Mature DHS—There is a need to strengthen the Department's ability to execute its mission responsibilities, run itself, and account for the resources that have been entrusted to it.

2

- Enhance Partner Capability and Capacity—Responsibilities for homeland security are broader than those of DHS and indeed broader than those of the Federal government. For that reason, there is a need to strengthen the ability of partners in the homeland security enterprise—in particular, State, local, tribal, and territorial governments, and the private sector—to execute important aspects of core homeland security mission activities.

- Deepen International Engagement—Finally, the security of our homeland begins far from our shores. We must work with key international partners to improve these critical partnerships and the activities that span the entire homeland security mission space, consistent with the broad range of U.S. Government international priorities and in consultation and coordination with the Department of State and the U.S. Chiefs of Mission in foreign countries.

The QHSR statute required an assessment of the organizational alignment of the Department with the national homeland security strategy and homeland security missions set forth in the QHSR Report. The BUR included this assessment. The BUR Report sets out initiatives and enhancements concerning DHS organization arising out of that assessment.

II. The Mission of the Department of Homeland Security

The Department of Homeland Security was formed in the wake of the terrorist attacks of September 11, 2001 as part of a deliberate and determined national effort to safeguard the United States against terrorism. In March 2003, DHS became the third-largest Federal department, bringing together all or part of 22 different Federal agencies, each with a role in safeguarding the United States against terrorism.

From the outset, however, the Department's mission responsibilities went well beyond preventing terrorism, and included response to and recovery from natural disasters, customs enforcement and collection of customs revenue, administration of legal immigration services, safety and stewardship of the Nation's waterways and marine transportation system, as well as other legacy missions of the various components of DHS. This breadth of mission responsibilities reflects the richness, history, and diversity of DHS components and the need to safeguard this country from a variety of threats and hazards.

In addition to combining 22 separate pre-existing entities, the creation of DHS included the establishment of a headquarters that includes management, science and technology, intelligence and analysis, policy, operations, and legal functions, specialty expertise in health affairs, domestic nuclear detection, and counternarcotics enforcement coordination, a citizenship and immigration services ombudsman, and the Federal Law Enforcement Training Center. DHS also placed a strong emphasis on cybersecurity and infrastructure protection within the National Protection and Programs Directorate. Annex A describes the main elements of the DHS force structure within the seven DHS operational components.

DHS headquarters also includes several offices with critical responsibilities for internal DHS coordination as well as communication and connection with the Department's external stakeholders, including public affairs, legislative affairs, intergovernmental affairs, State and local law enforcement, and the private sector, as well as offices focused on privacy, civil rights, and civil liberties. At DHS, clear and consistent communication with the general public, State, local, tribal, and territorial governments, as well as Congress is critical to advancing our priorities across a diverse and complex mission space from counterterrorism and countering violent extremism to individual, family, and community preparedness and resilience. Equally important, these offices ensure the Department's commitment to the preservation of privacy, civil rights, and civil liberties with respect to homeland security activities.

The mission of DHS is carried out through the tireless and dedicated efforts of more than 200,000 men and women who serve at the Department. As we act to strengthen and mature DHS and enhance our capability, DHS will ensure that its workforce is engaged in our mission, resilient, and properly trained. DHS will also continue to foster an environment where our employees understand the critical importance of their work and how their efforts contribute to the Department's goals. Annex B sets forth the range of DHS activities on any given day.

Integrating the many disparate entities of DHS—some with long histories of independent or autonomous operations, and all with distinct operational cultures—while maintaining their unique strengths and capabilities has presented significant public policy and management challenges. DHS recognizes the difficulty of this task, and through the QHSR and BUR processes has sought to deliberately and incrementally move DHS towards a more unified and integrated posture.

III. Enhancing Mission Performance

A. Preventing Terrorism and Enhancing Security

Current Authorities

Under the Homeland Security Act of 2002, the primary mission of the Department of Homeland Security begins with preventing terrorist attacks within the United States and reducing the vulnerability of the United States to terrorism. The Homeland Security Act specifies that the Secretary of Homeland Security is responsible for preventing the entry of terrorists and the instruments of terrorism into the United States. The act requires the Secretary to access, receive, and analyze law enforcement information, intelligence information, and other information from agencies of the Federal government, State and local government agencies (including law enforcement agencies), and private sector entities, and to integrate such information, in order to identify and assess the nature and scope of terrorist threats to the homeland; detect and identify threats of terrorism against the United States; and understand such threats in light of actual and potential vulnerabilities of the homeland.

The Homeland Security Act also makes the Secretary of Homeland Security responsible for coordinating overall efforts to manage risk to critical infrastructure and key resources; Homeland Security Presidential Directive 7 reinforces and describes this authority. The Secretary of Homeland Security is also vested with a range of authorities relating to chemical, biological, radiological, and nuclear (CBRN) countermeasures, biosurveillance, domestic nuclear detection, transportation of hazardous materials, chemical facility security, as well as broad customs authorities to prevent the importation of dangerous materials, including CBRN weapons and materials. The Aviation and Transportation Security Act of 2001, the Maritime Transportation Security Act of 2002, the Intelligence Reform and Terrorism Protection Act of 2004, and the SAFE Port Act of 2006 authorize a range of aviation, maritime, and surface transportation system security activities aimed at the deterrence, detection, and disruption of terrorist activities against the transportation sector, and Title 18 of the United States Code vests the Department, through the U.S. Secret Service, with responsibilities for protecting the President, the Vice President, national leaders, foreign heads of state and government, as well as certain facilities and events.

Overview of the DHS Role

Protecting the United States and its people from terrorism is the cornerstone of homeland security. This mission includes three goals:

(1) Preventing terrorist attacks;
(2) Preventing the unauthorized acquisition or use of CBRN materials and capabilities within the United States; and
(3) Reducing the vulnerability of critical infrastructure to terrorist attacks and other hazards.

DHS shares the responsibility to prevent terrorist attacks with several Federal departments and agencies. The Departments of State, Justice, and Defense, the Federal Bureau of Investigation (FBI), and the National Counterterrorism Center (NCTC) all have leadership roles and responsibilities in the U.S. government's efforts to prevent terrorist attacks. For example, the NCTC maintains the Terrorist Identities Datamart Environment (TIDE). The FBI administers the Terrorist Screening Center, which determines which individuals will be placed into the Terrorist Screening Database—the comprehensive terrorist watchlist—and administers the process by which the No Fly and Selectee lists are derived. The FBI and the Department of Justice also lead terrorism investigations; coordinate law enforcement efforts to detect, prevent, and disrupt terrorist attacks against the United States; and are responsible for the related intelligence collection activities within the United States. DHS operates as a principal consumer of NCTC and FBI watchlist products for DHS border and aviation security operations and vetting of key transportation workers. Also, DHS is a partner in data sharing and threat analysis, and supports the NCTC and national network of the FBI Joint Terrorism Task Forces. DHS intelligence entities—including intelligence elements within several DHS operational components—gather, share, and disseminate intelligence between the field and the larger Intelligence Community.

In support of several recent, high-profile counterterrorism investigations, DHS institutionalized an integrated DHS Threat Task Force (DTTF), composed of staff from multiple operational components of the Department who work alongside analysts from the Office of Intelligence and Analysis. The DTTF directly supports FBI investigations, ensures coordination across DHS, expedites cross-checking of Departmental data holdings for the National Targeting Center and other purposes, and provides time-urgent threat information to DHS leadership and, in coordination with the FBI, frontline law enforcement.

<u>Preventing Terrorist Attacks</u>

Within the context of coordination and collaboration with State, local, tribal, and territorial governments, nongovernmental organizations, and the private sector, the Department is charged with assisting State, local and private sector entities in disrupting potential terrorist activity and denying terrorists access to the United States at our land, air and sea ports of entry, as well as travel networks into and within the country.

DHS has adopted a multi-faceted approach to enhance aviation security capabilities both at home and abroad. DHS has the lead in three areas: (1) pursuing enhanced screening technology, protocols, and procedures, especially regarding aviation and other transportation sectors, consistent with privacy rights, civil rights, and civil liberties; (2) strengthening international partnerships and coordination on aviation security issues; and (3) developing recommendations on long-term law enforcement requirements for aviation security in coordination with the Department of Justice. In addition, DHS supports the Intelligence Community's efforts to re-evaluate and modify the criteria and processes used to create watchlists.

DHS devotes significant frontline resources to preventing terrorists from traveling to and within the United States and seizing prohibited materials that they may use in an attack. Through such activities as terrorist watchlists and targeting systems for vetting of passengers, physical screening of passengers and crew, baggage, and cargo, patrol and surveillance of our nation's borders, and counter proliferation and financial crimes investigations and substantial support to the FBI Joint Terrorism Task Forces, DHS attempts to deter, detect, mitigate, and prevent terrorist attacks on the homeland. TSA is working to improve security in the surface modes of transportation by performing risk assessments, closing vulnerability gaps, vetting key workers, providing training, conducting exercises, and deploying Visible Intermodal Prevention and Response teams (VIPRs).

DHS responsibilities for preventing terrorist attacks include assisting State, local, tribal, and territorial governments to obtain the information and capabilities to address threats. To this end, DHS awards almost $4 billion annually to State, local, tribal, and territorial governments through the State Homeland Security Grant Program, the Urban Areas Security Initiative, and other grant programs. These grant programs help State, local, tribal, and territorial governments build and sustain capabilities necessary to prevent terrorist attacks, as well as address other threats, prepare for, respond to, and recover from all hazards, and build additional public safety capability.

One prime example of these State, local, tribal, and territorial capabilities are fusion centers, which receive pertinent threat and risk information and analysis from the Intelligence Community and other Federal entities while also helping States and major municipalities collect, aggregate, fuse, and disseminate homeland security-related intelligence, law enforcement, and risk information to frontline officers and first responders, as well as back to the Intelligence Community and other Federal partners. In close partnership with this network of fusion centers, DHS plays a key role in preventing terrorist attacks that originate from within the United States.

Preventing the Unauthorized Acquisition or Use of CBRN Materials and Capabilities

While a variety of Federal departments and agencies are responsible for preventing the unauthorized acquisition or use of CBRN materials and capabilities, DHS plays a critical role in integrating these activities through programs implemented by U.S. Customs and Border Protection (CBP), the U.S. Coast Guard (USCG), the Domestic Nuclear Detection Office (DNDO), the Science and Technology Directorate (S&T), and other Departmental elements. DHS secures global trade and travel systems, investigates criminal activities involving the unlawful import and export of CBRN materials, technologies and capabilities, and detects and counters the importation and movement of CBRN weapons and materials into or already within the United States. In particular, the threat of nuclear terrorism is fundamentally unlike any of the other threats that DHS must prevent. The potential consequences of an attack using an improvised nuclear device require that the Department maintain a continued focus on prevention.

DHS prevents weapons of mass destruction and weapons of mass effect from entering the United States at and between ports of entry, investigates violations relating to the importation of CBRN materials, and regulates the security of high-risk chemical facilities. DHS has a specific focus on coordinating Federal efforts to detect and protect against the unauthorized importation, possession, storage, transportation, development, or use of a nuclear explosive device, fissile material, or radiological material in the United States. In addition, through the BioWatch program, which deploys sensor technology to detect the presence of biological agents, DHS coordinates with Federal, State, local, tribal, and territorial partners for management of biological attacks. DHS also provides substantial financial support and technical assistance to State, local, tribal, and territorial governments through grant programs for CBRN detection.

Managing Risks to Critical Infrastructure, Key Leadership, and Events

DHS has national leadership responsibilities for managing risks to critical infrastructure, key resources, and events. The Secretary of Homeland Security is vested by statute and Presidential directive with coordinating national efforts to secure and protect critical infrastructure and key resources, which the Department does currently through the National Protection and Programs Directorate (NPPD). Through communication and coordination with governmental and private sector partners, DHS leads the national effort to mitigate terrorism risk to, strengthen the protection of, and enhance the all-hazard resilience of the Nation's critical infrastructure across the identified 18 sectors. DHS is also the Sector-Specific Agency for 11 of the 18 critical infrastructure sectors set forth in the *National Infrastructure Protection Plan*: Chemical, Commercial Facilities, Communications, Critical Manufacturing, Dams, Emergency Services, Government Facilities, Information Technology, Nuclear Reactors, Materials and Waste, Postal and Shipping, and Transportation Systems. The U.S. Secret Service (USSS) has critical responsibilities for criminal investigations relating to the integrity of the financial system and the counterfeiting of U.S. currency. In addition, U.S. Immigration and Customs Enforcement (ICE) targets the underlying cross-border financial systems that terrorist and transnational criminal organizations may exploit in raising, moving, and storing illicit funds. ICE also seeks to deny transnational criminal organizations access to these systems. Annex E sets forth the 18 critical infrastructure sectors and the Sector-Specific Agency for each.

Through the Secret Service, DHS also has the unique responsibility to protect the President, the Vice President, visiting heads of state, and major Presidential candidates, as well as to ensure the continuity of national leadership. Protection includes all activities related to identifying threats, mitigating vulnerabilities, and creating secure environments wherever protectees work, reside, and travel. The Secret Service also coordinates protective intelligence investigations through its network of field offices and leads the design and implementation of operational security plans and protective activity for National Special Security Events. The Secret Service also has critical responsibilities for criminal investigations relating to the integrity of the financial systems and counterfeiting of United States currency.

Initiatives and Enhancements

The QHSR and BUR analyses suggest several priority initiatives, as well as enhancements to current programs, in order to better prevent terrorism and enhance security. Innovations like the DTTF represent a major step forward in coordinating counterterrorism activities, but DHS must find ways to further centralize coordination to leverage operational, intelligence, and strategic synergies across the department. Similarly, DHS must better leverage the critical information it receives across a wide range of mission-based and functional activities, while protecting privacy, civil rights, and civil liberties. Recent aviation security successes have laid the groundwork for further and necessary improvements in technology, process, and partnerships, and these efforts must remain an urgent mission priority. As threats evolve and complexity increases across the homeland security enterprise, standardization has become critically important. While our partnerships for critical infrastructure protection remain strong and continue to grow, we must strive to more effectively push information and knowledge out to the field where it is most urgently needed.

To address these challenges, the Department will strengthen counterterrorism coordination across DHS, strengthen land, maritime, and aviation security both domestically and abroad, create an integrated Departmental information sharing architecture, deliver infrastructure protection and resilience capabilities to the field, set national performance standards for identity verification, and increase efforts to detect and counter nuclear and biological weapons and dangerous materials. We will also enhance partner capability and capacity—particularly at the State, local, tribal, and territorial level—by standardizing and institutionalizing the National Fusion Center Network, pursue initiatives to safeguard access to secure areas in critical facilities, make DHS a center of excellence for canine training and deployment, and redesign the Federal Protective Service (FPS) to become a model critical infrastructure protection and law enforcement agency for the government sector and better match mission requirements.

- *Strengthen counterterrorism coordination across DHS.* Although DHS is one of the Federal government's key counterterrorism agencies, beyond the Secretary and Deputy Secretary, DHS did not have a single coordinating entity for counterterrorism activities. DHS recently designated a Coordinator for Counterterrorism who is responsible for coordinating all counterterrorism activities for the Department and across its directorates, components, and offices. DHS will continue to evolve the Counterterrorism coordination function in consultation with Congress.

- *Strengthen aviation security.* The attempted terrorist attack on Flight 253 on December 25, 2009, illustrates the continuing and evolving nature of the threat to the aviation transportation system. DHS has lead responsibilities for aviation security and is also embarking on a major global initiative to improve aviation security technology and processes around the world. DHS is also partnering with the Department of Energy—including the National Laboratories—and private industry to develop new and more effective technologies to deter and disrupt known threats and proactively anticipate and protect against new ways by which terrorists could seek to board an aircraft. DHS will also collaborate with the aviation industry to use a risk-based approach to inform decisions about changes to operations, business processes, and aircraft development. In all cases, DHS will use current intelligence-derived threat information to drive day-to-day operations. DHS will also work with other Federal, State, local, tribal, and territorial law enforcement partners and airport authorities to implement long-term, sustainable aviation security law enforcement. State, local, tribal, and territorial law enforcement and airport authorities play a critical role in our aviation security success.

- *Create an integrated Departmental information sharing architecture.* Given its daily interaction with the global movement of people and goods, DHS is uniquely authorized and positioned to fuse and analyze intelligence, law enforcement, screening, and other information gathered through encounters with travelers and commercial entities in order to prevent terrorist travel, finance, and operations. While the establishment of the DHS Threat Task Force was a step forward in data sharing, more work can be done to enhance DHS' ability to access information in near-real time and use it to identify people and goods posing high risk to the United States while protecting privacy, civil rights, and civil liberties. In order to accomplish this goal, DHS will create an information sharing architecture to consolidate and streamline access to intelligence, law enforcement, screening, and other information across the Department. That architecture will include the capability for automated recurrent screening and vetting for individuals to whom DHS has provided a license, privilege, or status (including immigration status) so that, as new information becomes available, DHS can assess whether the individual is no longer eligible for the benefit or presents a threat. It will also include the capability to conduct scenario-based automated targeting of individuals and other entities using intelligence-driven criteria.

- *Deliver infrastructure protection and resilience capabilities to the field.* Develop, deliver and continuously update a portfolio of DHS and Federal agency-wide capabilities, tools and products (e.g. from our partners in the Sector Specific Agencies) for critical infrastructure protection and resilience to State, local, tribal and territorial government and their local and regional partners and the private sector, tailored and supported based on regional and local needs. DHS will conduct these activities as it explores opportunities with the private sector to "design-in" greater resilience for critical infrastructure as described in "Ensuring Resilience to Disasters," below.

- *Set national performance standards for identification verification.* In order to meet the 9/11 Commission's recommendation regarding the security of State drivers' licenses and identification cards, DHS has supported the efforts of Governors and Congress to enact the *Providing for Additional Security in States' Identification Act* (PASS ID). PASS ID puts States on the path to implementing national standards for identification documents and will strengthen security across the country while enhancing privacy safeguards and protection of personally identifiable information. Although the May 2011 deadline for full compliance with the REAL ID Act remains in effect, legislative action is needed to address systemic problems with REAL ID to advance our security interests over the long term. DHS is committed to moving forward both administratively and with Congress to implement this key 9/11 Commission recommendation to help prevent terrorism, reduce fraud, and improve the reliability and accuracy of personal identification documents.

- *Increase efforts to detect and counter nuclear and biological weapons and dangerous materials.* DHS will prioritize nuclear detection research and development and also work with the Intelligence Community to develop intelligence and analysis capabilities relating to improvised nuclear devices and radiological dispersal devices, to include developing the capability to detect and react to pre-detonation cues or signatures to provide early-warning indicators of an imminent or credible threat of a terrorist attack using a nuclear weapon. DHS, working with its partners in the interagency, will also use the most advanced tools to facilitate investigations against vendors, buyers, and traders who violate export control laws and unlawfully transfer nuclear and biological technology over the Internet or controlled material of select agents anywhere. In addition, DHS will place greater emphasis on biological detection and countermeasures and accelerate development of forensics capabilities for biological weapons in order to help attribute those attacks to a particular country or group. These efforts will include increasing the capabilities of the DHS National Biodefense Analysis and Countermeasures Center (NBACC), which carries out many of these activities. DHS will also look to increase its international capabilities to track the evolution and migration of potentially high-consequence human, animal, and plant diseases.

- *Leverage the full range of capabilities to address biological and nuclear threats.* As noted above, in addition to increasing efforts to detect and counter nuclear and biological weapons and dangerous materials, DHS will increase its leadership role in protecting against biological and nuclear threats more generally. The DHS Office of Health Affairs (OHA) and the Domestic Nuclear Detection Office (DNDO) each bring critical capabilities to this effort. OHA concentrates mainly on chemical and biological threats and their consequences. DNDO focuses on detecting the presence of nuclear weapons and materials through implementation of the Global Nuclear Detection Architecture and assistance with attribution of interdicted nuclear material through the National Technical Nuclear Forensics Center. DHS will leverage these capabilities, while enhancing coordination with Federal, State, local, tribal, territorial, nongovernmental, and private sector partners on CBRN issues.

- *Standardize and institutionalize the National Fusion Center Network.* Since 2003, a national network of fusion centers has developed at the State, local, tribal, and territorial level, supported by funding, training, exercises, and technical assistance from DHS and the Department of Justice. However, to date, there has been no systematic effort to ensure that these centers establish and maintain a baseline level of capability so that they are able to become fully integrated into national efforts to gather, analyze, and share information needed to protect our communities. DHS has proposed a new National Fusion Center Program Management Office to assess the current level of capability of fusion centers and to support their meeting defined outcomes, national standards, and baseline levels of capability with Federal, State, local, tribal, and territorial partners, and the private sector.

- *Promote safeguards for access to secure areas in critical facilities.* Employees or other trusted or credentialed individuals who harbor malicious intentions present a pernicious challenge to safeguarding access to secure areas in critical facilities such as airports. To protect against this threat, DHS will expand risk-informed screening and recurrent vetting in the transportation sector to include additional populations of aviation and surface transportation workers in order to validate both the identity and the integrity of individuals with access to critical or sensitive infrastructure. DHS will also implement processes to recurrently vet all Federal employees, contractors, and Federal secure identification credential holders.

- *Establish DHS as a center of excellence for canine training and deployment.* Canines serve essential roles in homeland security. Specially-trained canines and their handlers are essential elements of terrorism prevention efforts at the Federal, State, local, tribal, and territorial levels and in the private sector. Canines also serve essential roles in detecting narcotics at the air, sea, and land ports of entry, and in search and rescue activities following disasters. DHS will increase specialized breeding activities for canines, enhance its training and certification of canines and handlers, and become a center of excellence for employment of canines across the homeland security missions.

- *Redesign the Federal Protective Service (FPS) to better match mission requirements.* FPS is responsible for protecting most facilities occupied or secured by the Federal government and the people in those facilities through the application of law enforcement and physical security authorities. (FPS is not responsible for certain Federal facilities, including military facilities such as the Pentagon.) In 2009, DHS transferred responsibility for FPS from ICE to NPPD. DHS now proposes to undertake a major redesign of FPS, in coordination with the U.S. General Services Administration, to set the future vision for FPS and define roles and responsibilities consistent with the fulfillment of this vision. The FPS redesign will create functional alignment within FPS and between FPS and other elements of DHS, better match mission requirements to the risk profiles of both leased and owned public buildings and infrastructure nationwide, and set FPS on a course to become a model critical infrastructure protection and law enforcement agency. Such an effort entails the realignment of the workforce to better match mission needs and customer expectations. Inherent in this effort is the need for a more capable Federal workforce, exploration of additional authorities, an increased use of innovative security technologies, and an examination of the optimal funding mechanism for securing and protecting facilities occupied by the Federal government.

B. Securing and Managing Our Borders

Current Authorities

Under the Homeland Security Act, the Secretary of Homeland Security is responsible for securing the borders, territorial waters, ports, terminals, waterways, and air, land, and sea transportation systems of the United States. This authority includes administration of the customs laws of the United States, and responsibility for ensuring the speedy, orderly, and efficient flow of people, goods, and information. The DHS is also responsible for monitoring connections between illegal drug trafficking and terrorism, coordinating efforts to sever such connections, and otherwise contributing to efforts to interdict illegal drug trafficking and its ill-gotten proceeds. The Immigration and Nationality Act of 1952, as amended, provides authority for the enforcement of the immigration laws to include immigration inspections and human smuggling interdiction at ports of entry as well as for the U.S. Border Patrol, part of CBP. Titles 14 and 19 of the United States Code provides broad customs enforcement authorities for securing and managing the movement of merchandise, people, conveyances, containers, and mail into and out of the United States, and the Tariff Act of 1930, as amended, provides that Customs officers enforce all laws relating to the assessment and collection of customs duties and related responsibilities. The Ports and Waterways Safety Act of 1972 and the SAFE Port Act of 2006 provide authorities for securing seaports and the international supply chain, as well as broad authority for the interrelated functions of promoting vessel safety and the protection of the marine environment; the Aviation and Transportation Security Act of 2001 provides authorities to protect the air transportation system. Homeland Security Presidential Directive 11 vests the Secretary of Homeland Security with leadership responsibilities for coordinating screening of people and cargo, and Homeland Security Presidential Directives 13 and 16 vest the Secretary of Homeland Security with leadership responsibilities for maritime and aviation security, respectively.

Overview of the DHS Role

We are responsible for secure, well-managed borders that not only protect the United States against threats from abroad, but also expedite the safe flow of lawful travel and commerce. Achieving this outcome depends on achieving three interrelated goals: (1) effectively securing U.S. air, land, and sea borders; (2) safeguarding lawful trade and travel; and (3) disrupting and dismantling transnational criminal organizations.

Working with our partners both nationally and internationally, our strategy is to manage and secure our Nation's borders by employing and enhancing our layers of security through the continuum that impacts our borders—starting from the point of origin overseas where people and cargo originate, through transit to the United States, the arrival and entry at our borders, then on to the routes of egress away from the border and ultimately to the final destination within the United States. This strategy relies upon using increased intelligence and risk management strategies in order to segment, sort, target, triage, and expedite the movement and flow of travelers and trade. We must constantly reevaluate and improve our effectiveness along each step of this continuum to ensure that we continue to be proactive in our approach to the security of our Nation.

Effectively Securing U.S. Air, Land, and Sea Borders

The border environment is characterized by three different areas of activity: (1) ports of entry, such as airports, seaports, and land border crossings; (2) areas between ports of entry; and (3) the approaches to our borders—the areas leading up to and surrounding U.S. borders. The border environment also includes those areas over which DHS components assert, exercise, and enforce legal jurisdiction (e.g. U.S. Territorial Sea, Contiguous Zone, Exclusive Economic Zone, and on U.S. vessels on the high seas). DHS relies on a combination of people, technology, and infrastructure (e.g. roads, fences) across DHS operating components to secure the border.

Through CBP and the U.S. Coast Guard (USCG), DHS is responsible for securing and enforcing U.S. law at the Nation's international borders, as well as at the over 300 official Ports of Entry, international mail facilities, and other points of entry to the United States. Along these borders and at these entry points, DHS is the key interface for America's international trading partners, for travelers seeking to enter or leave the United States, and for businesses seeking to import or export goods into or out of the United States. DHS also defends against transnational criminal or terrorist organizations seeking to exploit vulnerabilities in our open society, smuggle dangerous people, weapons, or goods into or out of our country, or attack critical border infrastructure.

At ports of entry in the air domain (airports with international flight arrivals), land domain (land border crossings), and maritime domain (seaports), DHS is responsible for physically screening people and goods upon their arrival to the country. DHS's work begins well before people and goods arrive at our borders. Using a variety of intelligence, automated tools, and information collected in advance of arrival for passengers and cargo, DHS works to screen, identify, and intercept threats at points of departure before they reach our shores. DHS conducts these activities in conjunction with international partners and the private sector through CBP-led programs such as the Container Security Initiative and Immigration Advisory Program. Similarly, through USCG, the Department ensures vessel security and compliance with both domestic and international safety and security standards through imposing Conditions of Entry on vessels and enforcing 96-hour Advance Notice of Arrival requirements. These programs ensure the security and resilience of the key global systems and networks essential to the U.S. and global economies.

Between ports of entry—where in the land domain all flows are by definition illegal—agents, technology, and infrastructure combined with a defense in-depth enforcement strategy are all key components of effective border security. DHS uses air, land, and marine assets to patrol and secure U.S. borders, as well as sophisticated systems to effectively detect and interdict potential threats beyond our borders. USCG provides air and maritime patrols along the U.S. border, including seacoasts, lakes, and rivers, where USCG and CBP have explicit legal authorities to enforce a broad array of U.S. laws designed to safeguard, secure, and protect U.S. citizens, vessels, and resources. In the approaches to the United States, CBP and USCG both maintain domain awareness efforts to establish and maintain situational awareness and a common operating picture of people, vehicles, aircraft, and marine vessels approaching our borders. Additionally, larger, more capable USCG afloat and air assets maintain an offshore presence to actively monitor offshore activity and engage when necessary to execute a layered approach to securing our maritime borders. DHS works closely with other Federal departments and agencies, such as the Departments of Justice, Transportation, and Defense, in conducting these activities. Effective, real-time coordination of interagency activities is critical for success in this cross-domain environment.

Safeguarding Lawful Travel and Trade

DHS plays an essential role in safeguarding lawful travel and trade. To do so most effectively, we must seek ways to interdict threats at the earliest point through international partnerships, better use of technology, and increased intelligence. Equally critical to ensuring the health of our economy is the need to enable the secure, lawful flow of people and goods into and out of the United States. DHS efforts entail both foreign and domestic activities and focus on the global trade and travel system and the risk posed by people and goods in transit.

Through the Transportation Security Administration (TSA), USCG, ICE, and CBP, DHS is active in global standard-setting organizations—such as the International Civil Aviation Organization, the International Maritime Organization, and the World Customs Organization—to create global standards for security and resilience of global trade and travel systems. In addition, TSA conducts inspections of foreign airports with direct flights to the United States in order to ensure adherence to international and TSA aviation security standards. Domestically, TSA regulates security of airports, including those with international arrivals, and CBP and USCG secure seaports and land ports of entry. USCG works closely with foreign navies and coast guards to enhance the inherent maritime port security capabilities of trading partners, in addition to regularly visiting foreign ports to ensure port facility security measures meet international standards.

CBP works with international customs and border agencies, as well as the trade community (including shippers, importers, brokers, and bonding companies), to ensure the security and integrity of foreign transactions and exchanges along global supply chains. This includes facilitating the flow of legitimate trade across U.S. borders while securing our borders and helping to protect the American economy from illicit commercial enterprises. This includes helping to protect American businesses from theft of intellectual property and unfair trade practices, enforcing trade laws related to admissibility, and protecting the American public from health and public safety threats.

DHS components work to secure modes of transportation and their crews. TSA works with domestic and foreign airlines, as well as aircraft manufacturers, to ensure the integrity of aircraft and air crews, and works with the air cargo supply chain to ensure the integrity of cargo transported on passenger aircraft. USCG regulates vessel owners and operators and conducts regular inspections for safety and security purposes. CBP works with shippers to ensure the integrity of international shipments and cargo containers and vets crew members of vessels and passenger ships.

DHS also plays an important role in managing the risk of people and goods in transit to the United States. DHS maintains databases of information consistent with privacy, civil rights, and civil liberties safeguards, enforcing security standards for travel documents, and detecting the use of fraudulent documents in order to identify terrorists, criminals, and other risks. Through the Secure Flight program, DHS will ensure consistency in the vetting of domestic and international passengers against terrorist databases. Through resources such as the National Targeting Center, DHS screens people, goods, and conveyances bound for the United States through air, land, and sea routes, and provides information to agents and officials on the ground to intercept known and suspected threats. DHS also posts officers to foreign ports and works collaboratively with foreign countries, port operators, and shipping companies to screen cargo, investigate visa applications, and collaborate on aviation security. While the Department of State adjudicates and issues visas abroad, DHS—primarily through its visa security units—works closely with the Department of State in many countries where applicants present the highest threat in order to reduce the risk of terrorist or transnational criminals receiving a visa.

Through an automated risk assessment process, CBP screens 100 percent of all arriving cargo using advanced manifest data. Shipments posing a potential risk are identified prior to departure for maritime cargo, and prior to arrival into the U.S. port of entry for air and land cargo. Maritime cargo identified as high risk may be examined overseas, as part of the Container Security Initiative, which is in operation at 58 seaports worldwide, representing over 80 percent of the maritime cargo destined for the U.S. worldwide. At U.S. ports of entry, CBP uses radiation portal monitors to scan arriving cargo for radiation. Currently, 100 percent of the cargo and vehicle traffic at our land ports of entry and 99.3 percent of containerized maritime cargo at our seaports are scanned. TSA will implement 100 percent screening of air cargo on passenger aircraft traveling point-to-point domestically and departing from the U.S. for foreign destinations by August 2010, and is working with the international air cargo community to increase screening of air cargo on inbound international passenger aircraft.

As an interrelated function with respect to lawful trade, the Department, through CBP, also proactively facilitates trade and collects over $34 billion in customs revenue each year for the United States treasury.

Disrupting and Dismantling Transnational Criminal and Terrorist Organizations

DHS is the Federal government's largest law enforcement department. CBP and ICE have broad investigatory and enforcement authorities that cover not only immigration violations but also a wide range of border-related crime, including violations of U.S. customs, import, and export control laws. ICE investigates violations of over 400 statutes that protect the U.S. against the unlawful entry and export of people, goods, and monetary instruments. ICE works closely with other DHS law enforcement agencies, such as CBP, TSA, and USSS, as well as with other Federal law enforcement agencies, such as the FBI, the Drug Enforcement Administration, the Bureau of Alcohol, Tobacco, Firearms, and Explosives, and the U.S. Postal Inspection Service to investigate transnational criminal organizations that engage in smuggling and trafficking across the U.S. border. Human smuggling and trafficking, child sex tourism, counter proliferation, financial, intellectual property, weapons trafficking, and narcotics investigations are among ICE's top investigative priorities. DHS conducts investigations through its Border Enforcement Security Taskforces (BESTs) and Integrated Border Enforcement Teams (IBETs) that combine CBP and ICE agents and officers with Federal, State, local, tribal, and territorial law enforcement partners, as well as international partners, to interdict illegal drug trafficking, detect and disrupt illicit pathways used by transnational criminal and terrorist organizations, and arrest foreign nationals attempting to enter the United States illegally.

Initiatives and Enhancements

The QHSR and BUR analyses presented several opportunities for improvement. While effective mechanisms exist for interagency and intra-Departmental operational and intelligence coordination, we must learn from the successes of Joint Interagency Task Force-South (JIATF-South) and other similar constructs to further integrate and enhance domain awareness across our efforts to secure the border and expedite lawful travel and trade. Our investigations portfolio focused on transnational criminal and terrorist organizations must reflect our priorities and adopt a more proactive posture. We must do more to directly support key international partners in their efforts, both with respect to training and technical assistance, and direct coordination, information sharing, and joint risk assessments.

Therefore, in order to strengthen efforts to secure and manage our borders, the Department will seek to expand joint operations and intelligence capabilities, including enhanced domain awareness, prioritize immigration and customs investigations on the security of global trade and travel systems, enhance the security of global trade and travel systems, expand DHS international border integrity and customs enforcement security assistance, and work closely with the governments of Canada and Mexico to enhance North American security.

- *Expand joint operations and intelligence capabilities, including enhanced domain awareness.* DHS will unify the uses of technology, surveillance capabilities, and related resources across air, land, and maritime domains, with an increased emphasis on data collection, data processing, and integrating sensors across domains. DHS will harmonize operations and intelligence—utilizing concepts and structures modeled after JIATF-South, as appropriate—for the geographical approaches not covered by JIATF-South, such as the southwest border, as well as for arrivals of people and goods into the United States. Working with its partners, including the Department of Justice and the Office of National Drug Control Policy, DHS also will build upon the successful models established as part of our interagency counternarcotics infrastructure—including the Air and Marine Operations Center, the El Paso Intelligence Center, and other DHS and U.S. government operations centers—to apply those models more broadly to the spectrum of homeland security challenges across the air, land, and maritime domains. Finally, DHS will establish and coordinate cross-domain operational threat analysis and response protocols in order to ensure greater effectiveness of interagency and intergovernmental response to threats across air, land, and maritime domains.

- *Prioritize immigration and customs investigations on the security of global trade and travel systems.* DHS law enforcement agencies have substantial authorities to disrupt and dismantle transnational criminal and terrorist organizations that seek to exploit lawful trade and travel systems and establish illicit pathways for the movement of people and goods. DHS will strategically prioritize investigations to focus proactively on security of the global trade and travel system that directly affect immigration and customs activity across U.S. borders. Priorities within this proactive investigative portfolio will include human smuggling and trafficking, child sex tourism, counter proliferation, financial, intellectual property, weapons trafficking, and narcotics investigations.

- *Enhance the security and resilience of global trade and travel systems.* As described in the QHSR Report, securing and managing our borders is about more than the physical border environment. We must enable the secure, lawful flow of people and goods into and out of the United States. To that end, DHS will continue the development and implementation of trusted traveler and trusted shipper programs in order to increase our knowledge of people and goods that pose low risk traveling or transiting in global trade and travel systems. DHS will also enhance the sophistication of its information sharing architecture in order to evaluate the risk posed by people and goods in transit while safeguarding privacy, civil rights, and civil liberties. Trusted traveler and shipper programs and a more sophisticated information sharing architecture will allow DHS and its partners to focus information collection, targeting, and interdiction efforts on people and goods known or believed to pose high risk to the United States. To support these efforts, we will strengthen international information sharing agreements regarding criminals, terrorists, and individuals with suspected ties to terrorists and collaborate with the Department of State to institutionalize enhanced visa security programs at high-risk visa adjudication posts.

- *Strengthen and expand DHS-related security assistance internationally (e.g. border integrity and customs enforcement security assistance) consistent with U.S. government security, trade promotion, international travel, and foreign assistance objectives.* Our national security depends on the ability of foreign governments to effectively combat terrorism and other threats within their own borders. DHS has substantial capability and capacity to help implement assistance and training to foreign governments in areas such as biometrics, document fraud, aviation security, port and maritime security, cargo security, bulk cash smuggling, customs enforcement, and human smuggling and trafficking. The U.S. government, through the Departments of State and Defense, provides security assistance and foreign assistance to legitimate members and representatives of foreign security forces and civilian institutions. This includes providing resources to institutions related to homeland security in foreign countries—including land and maritime border integrity and customs enforcement functions. DHS believes that training and technical assistance for international security partners in the areas of border integrity and customs enforcement must be increased. DHS also supports the strengthening of security to facilitate travel and commerce for legitimate travelers and goods. DHS will work in consultation and coordination with the Departments and State and Defense, as well as with Congress, to ensure adequate resources to support these purposes. DHS will also coordinate a proposal with the Department of Defense (DOD) to post DHS liaison officers in each of the DOD geographic commands to coordinate and integrate homeland security-related assistance funding aims. Finally, DHS will explore the expansion of additional international partnerships for homeland security-related activities as appropriate, in consultation and coordination with the Department of State and, where appropriate, DOD, including current activities such as visa security and international law enforcement training.

- *Enhance North American security.* Our efforts to secure and manage our borders will be most effective when we work collectively with our North American partners, Canada and Mexico. To that end, DHS will enhance information sharing with Federal, State, local, tribal, nongovernmental, private sector, and international partners along the Northern and Southern borders. DHS will also foster cross-border threat and risk assessments and enhanced coordination and cooperation on securing the transnational flow of people and goods through expanding joint efforts and shared resources.

Our efforts to strengthen DHS intelligence and information sharing capabilities described above in the "Preventing Terrorism and Enhancing Security" section will also assist these efforts.

C. Enforcing and Administering Our Immigration Laws

Current Authorities

Pursuant to the Homeland Security Act, the Secretary of Homeland Security is responsible for establishing national immigration enforcement policies and priorities and administering the lawful immigration system, including establishing and administering rules governing the granting of visas, refugee, and asylum or other forms of permission to enter the United States. The Immigration and Nationality Act of 1952, as amended (INA), provides the Secretary with authority to administer the immigration laws of the United States as well as authority to arrest, detain, prosecute, and remove unauthorized foreign nationals present in the United States, especially those identified as criminals, fugitives, and otherwise dangerous. The INA confers authority to investigate civil and criminal violations of immigration laws, including human smuggling and fraud investigations.

Overview of the DHS Role

Smart and effective enforcement and administration of U.S. immigration laws allows the government to facilitate lawful immigration while identifying and removing those who violate our laws. Enforcing and administering our immigration laws depends on (1) strengthening and effectively administering our immigration system; and (2) preventing unlawful immigration.

Strengthening and Effectively Administering the Immigration Services System

As noted above, the Homeland Security Act of 2002 vests the Secretary of Homeland Security with the authority to set immigration and visa policy and administer the immigration system, with the INA serving as the basic immigration law of the United States. DHS works with other Federal departments and agencies in discharging these responsibilities, including the Departments of State, Justice, and Labor.

Multiple components within DHS share responsibility for executing immigration and visa policy. CBP, ICE, and U.S. Citizenship and Immigration Services (USCIS), along with USCG, the US-VISIT program within NPPD, and other organizational elements execute these responsibilities. Strengthening and effectively administering immigration services and adjudicative decisions—

whether they include determinations of eligibility, admissibility, or removability—requires collaborative efforts by all partners.

DHS, through USCIS, provides immigration and naturalization benefits, as well as asylum and other services to immigrants. The Citizenship and Immigration Services Ombudsman in DHS headquarters works to improve the delivery of immigration and citizenship services and assists the public in resolving difficult cases.

USCIS plays the principal role in adjudicating immigrant and nonimmigrant visa petitions, applications for adjustment of status, and requests for extensions of stay for tourists, students, business visitors, and other visitors. In addition, USCIS adjudicates applications for asylum and refugee status, petitions for intercountry adoption, and administers immigration benefits for other vulnerable populations such as victims of human trafficking, violent crimes, armed conflict, environmental disaster, and domestic violence. Effective administration of the immigration system depends on ensuring that immigration decisions are fair, lawful, and sound. In addition, the Department works with communities, other Federal departments and agencies, and nongovernmental organizations to promote the integration of lawful immigrants into American society. USCIS works with the Departments of Health and Human Services, Labor, State, and Housing and Urban Development on issues with overlapping jurisdiction.

Preventing Unlawful Immigration

In addition to administering the immigration system, DHS plays the lead role in preventing unlawful immigration. These activities include DHS's efforts to effectively secure U.S. air, land, and sea borders (discussed above), while removing foreign nationals who pose national security-related and other threats to the United States, or who are otherwise in the United States illegally.

ICE, working with USCIS and CBP, also plays a key role in preventing unlawful immigration through its investigative, intelligence, deterrence, and enforcement functions. But because barriers, screening, and enforcement operations alone cannot completely stop illegal immigration, systematic efforts to reduce the jobs magnet are necessary. Employers continue to hire workers who are not authorized to work—some knowingly and others unknowingly— because workers present fraudulent documents. Recent technological advances have improved identification of fraudulent documents and provide employers with tools to verify the work authorization status of newly hired employees.

DHS works to reduce demand for illegal immigrants by conducting inspections, audits, and investigations of employers who hire illegal immigrants and administers tools such as E-Verify and the Systematic Alien Verification for Entitlements (SAVE) system to facilitate compliance with immigration laws. The Department also works to eliminate systemic vulnerabilities by combating fraudulent applications for immigration services and by investigating fraudulent use of immigration documents to obtain other benefits or government services.

DHS works to prevent illegal entry by partnering with the Department of State both domestically and overseas to ensure that visas to enter the United States are not granted to foreign nationals who pose a threat to public safety or national security. These efforts complement U.S. border security efforts that prevent illegal entry both at and between ports of entry, described in the above section. DHS also works closely with the Departments of Justice and State as well as foreign governments and nongovernmental partner entities to share information used to combat alien smuggling and human trafficking.

Finally, ICE administers the detention and removal system by which foreign nationals found to be national security or public safety threats, criminals, or otherwise unlawfully present in the United States are arrested, detained, and removed from the United States. The Department works with the Department of Justice to ensure timely hearing of immigration cases and appeals, and with the JTTF with respect to foreign nationals who pose a national security threat.

Although immigration enforcement is constitutionally vested with the Federal government, DHS partners with State, local, tribal, and territorial law enforcement officers through the Secure Communities program to assist in identifying criminal foreign nationals and foreign nationals posing national security threats who are incarcerated. In addition, under the INA's Section 287(g) program, State, local, tribal, and territorial law enforcement agencies are granted limited authority, under Federal supervision and monitoring, to enforce Federal immigration laws.

Initiatives and Enhancements

The QHSR and BUR analyses make clear that achieving success in enforcing and administering our immigration laws will demand enhanced policies, targeted enforcement, and improved management of the system. Comprehensive legislative reform remains a fundamental necessity. We must continue to move beyond a paper-based application process and seek ways to standardize services, policies, and implementation throughout the system. Our ability to quickly analyze information, identify high-risk cases, and focus on fraud and national security concerns must continue to improve. We must continue to improve E-verify and find ways to promote and incentivize voluntary employer compliance. We must address fundamental issues related to our detention and removal efforts and build the detention system commensurate with the risk. Finally, new Americans need greater opportunities to become full members of their communities.

Based on DHS' responsibilities in this area, DHS will pursue comprehensive immigration reform, improve DHS immigration services processes, focus on fraud detection and national security vetting, target egregious employers who knowingly exploit illegal workers, dismantle human smuggling organizations, improve the detention and removal process and emphasize Secure Communities and efforts to identify and deport criminal aliens, ensure the integration of our newest Americans so that they become fully vested members of our Nation, and build and maintain a model detention system.

- *Comprehensive immigration reform.* Effective enforcement and administration of our immigration laws can best be built on comprehensive legislative reform that: (1) bolsters border security and interior enforcement; (2) mandates a nationwide employment verification program to stem the demand for illegal immigration and hold employers accountable for hiring unauthorized workers; (3) provides a mechanism to help clear family and employment visa backlogs; (4) recasts the legal migration provisions to better match the needs of the twenty-first century, for both high-skill and low-skill workers; and (5) carefully crafts a tough but fair program under which illegal immigrants will register, record biometrics, pass a criminal background check, pay any back taxes, pay a fine, learn English, and in return, be allowed to remain legally in the country and earn the opportunity for lawful permanent residence. Working closely with interagency partners and Congress, and in ongoing dialogue with external stakeholders from across the country, DHS will continue to develop and advance comprehensive immigration reform legislation.

- *Improve DHS immigration services processes.* Effective administration of the immigration system depends on fair, user-friendly processes and the identification and correction of vulnerabilities in real time. DHS will expedite the transformation of the immigration services system from a paper-based to an electronic-based application process. The Department will also ensure the standardization of immigration services policies and implementation across regions, offices, and agencies where applicable. DHS will also explore restructuring funding for USCIS to address variability in demand.

- *Focus on fraud detection and national security vetting.* DHS immigration authorities are powerful tools used against terrorists and other foreign nationals posing national security threats. DHS will improve its ability to analyze information, especially in identifying high risk cases, to better address fraud and national security concerns. DHS will strategically prioritize and manage investigations of interior immigration violations and visa overstays to target and remove criminal aliens and foreign nationals who pose a threat to national security, and increase intelligence relating to analysis of entry, exit, and stay information.

- *Target egregious employers who knowingly exploit illegal workers.* Preventing unlawful immigration depends in part on reducing the demand for illegal labor. DHS will seek legislative authority to increase civil and criminal penalties for employers who knowingly employ illegal aliens. Enhancing and expanding the E-Verify system is a critical component of ensuring a legal workforce. Additional work is underway to improve the accuracy of the system, combat identity fraud, address employer misuse, ensure that employees understand their rights, and allow employees to correct government records. While implementing E-Verify improvements and enhancing efforts to promote voluntary employer compliance, DHS will focus worksite enforcement on egregious employers who knowingly exploit illegal labor and critical infrastructure sites.

- *Dismantle human smuggling organizations.* Illegal immigration is facilitated by transnational criminal organizations that smuggle aliens internationally, across U.S. borders and within the interior of the country. DHS will enhance efforts to conduct investigations to dismantle these criminal organizations and will work with the Department of Justice to ensure successful prosecution of their leadership and forfeiture of their profits and other non-monetary assets or infrastructure. DHS will also work with the Department of Health and Human Services and other partners to implement best practices for processing undocumented, unaccompanied alien children who present themselves at the border.

- *Improve the detention and removal process.* As described above, DHS administers the detention and removal process through ICE in partnership with the Department of Justice. To improve the efficiency of this process, particularly as applied to criminal and other dangerous foreign nationals, DHS will increase non-investigatory law enforcement staffing for detention and removal operations to focus law enforcement on criminal investigations. DHS will continue to institutionalize the Secure Communities program to ensure enforcement resources are targeted based on risk, ensuring that criminal aliens are identified and processed efficiently for removal. DHS will also expand the Criminal Alien Program (CAP) at State, local, tribal, and territorial detention facilities to increase the number of criminal aliens who have removal orders by the time they complete their criminal sentence, removing the burden in detaining these aliens beyond their criminal sentences while awaiting removal orders. DHS will also seek to strengthen staffing at existing CAP sites, equip additional sites, and will work with DOJ to ensure that State, local, tribal, and territorial receipt of Federal detention funding is tied to participation in the Secure Communities (also known as a Comprehensive Plan to Identify and Remove Criminal Aliens (CIRCA)) and CAP programs.

- *Work with new Americans so that they fully transition to the rights and responsibilities of citizenship.* Effective integration of lawful immigrants supports an America where all individuals are secure in their rights, can exercise their civil liberties, and have opportunities to become full participants in their communities. Promoting integration also fosters a resilient public resistant to the enticements of extremism. DHS, with our interagency partners and stakeholders, will develop strategies that help new citizens integrate and assist eligible immigrants with naturalization. This includes core programs already underway in the public and nonprofit sectors, such as those provided by the Departments of Education and Health and Human Services. DHS will also increase its efforts to encourage legal permanent residents to become naturalized American citizens.

- *Maintain a model detention system commensurate with risk.* DHS will operate its detention system to ensure that the level of detention is commensurate with the risk posed by the detainees in its custody. Together with its partners and stakeholders, DHS will revise national standards for detainee care and treatment, including the treatment of families, minors, and those needing continuing medical treatment, ensure that detention facilities housing immigration detainees meet or exceed these standards, and cancel the contracts at facilities that receive deficient ratings. DHS will also take other steps in the near and long term to materially improve the immigration detention system. Those steps include: reducing the number of facilities DHS uses, issuing requests for proposals for new facilities commensurate with the risk posed by detainees, developing a detainee locator system to maximize communication between detainees and their families, strengthening the system that monitors the conditions within detention facilities, and ensuring the detainee health care system provides detainees with adequate and timely access to necessary care. DHS will also support increased funding for Alternatives to Detention (ATD).

D. Safeguarding and Securing Cyberspace

Current Authorities

As noted above, pursuant to the Homeland Security Act of 2002, the Secretary of Homeland Security is responsible for coordinating overall efforts to manage risk to critical infrastructure and key resources, including enhancing non-Federal cybersecurity. Homeland Security Presidential Directive 23, Cybersecurity Policy, provides that the Secretary shall lead the national effort to protect, defend, and reduce vulnerabilities of Federal systems (excluding civilian national security systems), and shall provide consolidated intrusion detection, incident analysis, and cyber response capabilities to protect Federal agencies' external access points. The May 2009 Cyberspace Policy Review outlined specific cybersecurity responsibilities to DHS. Additionally, the U.S. Secret Service is authorized by law to prevent, detect, and investigate electronic financial crimes, working closely with state and local law enforcement. The support for the Department's cybersecurity efforts is also embedded in the missions of Intelligence and Analysis, Science and Technology, and other offices and components.

Overview of the DHS Role

Cyber infrastructure forms the backbone of the Nation's economy and connects every aspect of our way of life. While the cyber environment offers the potential for rapid technological advancement and economic growth, a range of malicious actors seek to exploit cyberspace for dangerous or harmful purposes, disrupt communications or other services, and attack the Nation's infrastructure through cyberspace. We must secure the system of networks and information while promoting economic growth, protecting privacy, and sustaining civil rights and civil liberties.

Creating a Safe, Secure, and Resilient Cyber Environment

DHS leads the national effort to protect civilian government computer systems, in cooperation with the Office of Management and Budget (OMB) and the National Institute of Standards and Technology (NIST). DHS also works with industry to defend privately-owned and operated critical infrastructure and with State, local, tribal, and territorial governments to secure their systems.

To protect against current threats, DHS has the primary responsibility for working with civilian agencies and cyber centers across the Federal government, with State, local, tribal, and territorial governments, and with the private sector, to share information and collaborate to enable understanding of the threat, provide indications and warnings, and create common situational awareness utilizing and strengthening the public private partnership model established under the *National Infrastructure Protection Plan*. DHS collects and analyzes a wide variety of information regarding current and emerging cybersecurity threats and threat actors, and disseminates products to help improve the defensive posture of Federal agencies. DHS operates the National Cybersecurity and Communications Integration Center, which receives and analyzes reports of cyber incidents on Federal agency networks and provides warnings to Federal agencies, State, local, tribal, and territorial governments, and critical infrastructure owners and operators. DHS also operates the National Cyber Security Center, which promotes coordination and common situational awareness across Federal cybersecurity operations centers. Working through the councils of the *National Infrastructure Protection Plan*'s Sector Partnership, other Critical Infrastructure Partnerships and their unified public-private Information Sharing Environment, DHS, other Federal agencies, and State, local, tribal, and territorial governments, collaborate and share cybersecurity information with critical infrastructure owners and operators, to enhance understanding of the threat, situational awareness, prevention, and incident response. DHS also maintains an area of focus on the security of control systems, which manage the basic functions of significant elements of our infrastructure, in order to further resilience.

Similarly, DHS has the responsibility to support cyber risk management and reduction in the Federal civilian (excluding civilian national security systems) and State, local, tribal, and territorial government domains as well as in the private sector, to support their efforts to protect information systems, networks, personal and sensitive data, and to make systems and networks more resilient. Through the Trusted Internet Connection, EINSTEIN, and other programs, DHS is strengthening the defenses of Federal agency networks and enhancing protection of privacy by reducing their exposure to attacks, setting standards for security and network operations centers, and deploying intrusion sensors to detect and prevent attacks. In cooperation with the Department of Commerce and OMB, DHS develops and issues advisories and best practices to Federal agencies, helping to ensure that known vulnerabilities are addressed quickly and that preparations are made to mitigate emerging threats. Going forward, DHS will continue to support Federal civilian agencies and the private sector in meeting national and homeland security-related cybersecurity requirements—derived from standards, policy, and an understanding of the threat and necessary responses.

DHS is responsible for creating and maintaining a robust public-private cyber incident response capability to manage cyber incidents from identification to resolution in a rapid and replicable manner with prompt and appropriate action. DHS is responsible for coordinating effective response by Federal civilian agencies—as well as military and intelligence agencies as appropriate—and where necessary, directing appropriate mitigation; DHS also supports and coordinates with the private sector to enhance its response. To serve many of these purposes, DHS maintains the United States Computer Emergency Readiness Team (US-CERT), which is charged with providing response support and defense against cyber intrusions and attacks for Federal civilian networks (excluding civilian national security systems) as well as information sharing and collaboration with State, local, tribal, and territorial governments, industry, and international partners. US-CERT interacts with Federal agencies, industry, the research community, State, local, tribal, and territorial governments, and others to disseminate reasoned and actionable cybersecurity information to the public. US-CERT also provides a way for citizens, businesses, and other institutions to communicate and coordinate directly with the United States government about cybersecurity. DHS works closely with civilian, military, law enforcement, and intelligence agencies to ensure an integrated and holistic response.

DHS shares responsibility with other government agencies to prevent cyber crime and other malicious uses of cyberspace, by disrupting criminal organizations and other bad actors engaged in high-consequence or wide-scale cyber crime. DHS law enforcement components— particularly USSS and ICE—play key roles in investigating, disrupting, and deterring homeland security-related cyber crime, specifically, high-consequence or wide-scale crimes committed in cyberspace or against cyber networks, particularly in the financial, child exploitation, and intellectual property arenas, respectively, working closely with other Federal agencies and State, local, tribal, territorial, and international partners to disrupt criminal activity affecting U.S. assets. USSS has established a network of 29 domestic and international Electronic Crimes Task Forces (ECTF) to combine the resources of academia, the private sector, and Federal, State, local, tribal, and territorial law enforcement agencies to combat computer-based threats to U.S. financial systems and critical infrastructure—a capability that has allowed ECTFs to identify and address potential cyber vulnerabilities before criminals exploit them. ICE's Cyber Crimes Center investigates cyber crimes involving cross-border criminal activity, including child exploitation, identity, document, and benefit fraud, thefts of intellectual property, money laundering, commercial fraud, counterproliferation, and other cross-border criminal schemes.

In its efforts to promote cybersecurity, DHS benefits from the work of its Privacy Office and its Office for Civil Rights and Civil Liberties. For example, the Privacy Office has conducted, and made available to the public, reviews of the EINSTEIN program. Likewise, the Privacy Office has conducted a classified Privacy Impact Assessment of the exercise involving enhanced capabilities for the EINSTEIN program and information-sharing with the National Security Agency, and has made available to the public an unclassified version of that assessment in furtherance of the DHS commitment to transparency. Through the continuing work of these offices, DHS will ensure that the initiatives it undertakes to promote cybersecurity will protect privacy, civil rights, and civil liberties.

Promoting Cybersecurity Knowledge and Innovation

To protect against future threats, and to create a more secure cyber "ecosystem," DHS works broadly to raise awareness, build knowledge, drive innovation, and create the technical and governance foundation of stronger network security. DHS will also lead the Administration's National Cybersecurity Public Awareness Campaign, and is working with other Federal departments and agencies to build the cyber workforce of the future.

DHS plays a key role in supporting innovation by sponsoring technical and other research in the public and private sectors. Perhaps most important, as part of DHS' responsibility to enhance the protection of critical infrastructure, including the government, DHS is driving efforts to make the cyber ecosystem more secure by building standards and governance solutions that meet national and homeland security requirements. This includes automation of security to facilitate real-time response, interoperability to support security cooperation across sectors, and privacy-enhancing authentication so we can effectively protect our systems.

DHS, in partnership with the private sector, State, local, tribal, and territorial governments, and Federal agencies such as the Departments of Defense and Commerce, also encourages the enhancement of the security and integrity of the hardware, software, services, and architecture that will constitute a fundamentally more secure cyber ecosystem. DHS also supports research and development of emerging cybersecurity products and processes, working closely with industry and academia to bring promising new technology and techniques to increase the Nation's cybersecurity.

Initiatives and Enhancements

Given DHS's broad responsibility for Federal civilian (excluding civilian national security systems) and private sector networks and the priorities outlined in the QHSR, DHS's cybersecurity activities must be consolidated, coordinated, and strong. The line between physical and cyber critical infrastructure continues to blur, creating synergies across these activities that must be accounted for when considering our organizational and operational posture. Cybersecurity authorities across the Federal government have in many cases adapted well to a more networked world, but work remains to ensure clear lines of authority and mission. Adversaries continue to shift and refine tactics to penetrate our networks, placing high demand on our ability to anticipate, attribute, and prosecute cyber threats. Finally, though much progress has been made, efforts to maintain strong public awareness of the latest tactics and techniques and the optimal means of thwarting them must be continuously honed and improved.

For these reasons, DHS will undertake the following initiatives and enhancements to strengthen the Department's capabilities in cybersecurity—including creating a cybersecurity and infrastructure resilience operational component within DHS, strengthening DHS authorities and capabilities to protect cyber networks, increasing DHS cyber predictive, investigative, and forensic capabilities, and promoting cybersecurity public awareness.

- *Increase the focus and integration of DHS's operational cybersecurity and infrastructure resilience activities.* DHS has substantial operational cyber security responsibilities, which are inextricably intertwined with its responsibilities to manage all hazards risk to critical infrastructure. DHS typically manages its operational responsibilities through operating components. However, the majority of DHS's operational activities relating to cyber security and infrastructure protection and resilience are currently administered by the NPPD, which is designated as a DHS headquarters element. DHS will focus NPPD's activities on operations and more closely align cyber and critical infrastructure protection and resilience efforts, in cooperation with the private sector, to secure cyber networks and make critical infrastructure resilient. DHS will examine ways to clarify NPPD's increasingly operational role as opposed to other elements of the DHS headquarters, as well as NPPD's functions not related to cybersecurity or infrastructure protection and resilience.

- *Strengthen DHS ability to protect cyber networks.* DHS is responsible for the protection of Federal networks (the .gov domain), excluding civilian national security systems. However, further efforts are needed to effectively fulfill this responsibility. To this end, DHS will increase its cybersecurity activities for Federal civilian networks (excluding civilian national security systems) to ensure that national cybersecurity requirements are met, as well as additional resources to develop the capabilities necessary to effectively implement those authorities in close collaboration with other departments and agencies. In order to keep pace with emerging threats and new technologies, DHS will also seek to use new models for developing, acquiring, and disseminating cybersecurity technology, including technology leasing arrangements, technical service agreements, and development of secondary markets for cybersecurity technology among State, local, tribal, and territorial governments. Finally, DHS' effort to "design-in" greater resilience for critical infrastructure to ensure national security requirements are met will include a cybersecurity focus.

- *Increase DHS predictive, investigative, and forensic capabilities for cyber intrusions and attacks.* The ability to predict the emergence of new cyber threats will help mitigate the effects of such threats. Likewise, the ability to determine the source of a cyber attack, intrusion, or disruption both increases the likelihood of a successful prosecution of the attacker and creates a powerful deterrent effect against both state and non-state actors. To that end, DHS will build a new predictive analytic capability that will work closely with the law enforcement and intelligence communities and the private sector to improve the identification of cyber adversaries, establish and advance deterrence strategies, and promote a more accurate understanding of emerging cyber threats. To meet these goals, DHS will enhance its efforts to recruit and develop an expanded cyber intelligence and analysis team. DHS will also expand and prioritize investigative activities targeted at high-consequence or wide-scale cyber attacks, intrusions, and disruptions, and associated transborder cybersecurity-related crime, in cooperation with other law enforcement agencies through the National Cyber Investigative Joint Task Force. DHS will establish reliable mechanisms to categorize, store, and retrieve relevant cyber information from DHS databases, consistent with protection of privacy, civil rights, and civil liberties. Finally, DHS will develop and implement a robust process to share finished cyber intelligence products and other information in a timely fashion within DHS and with our Federal, State, local, tribal, territorial, and private sector partners.

- *Promote cybersecurity public awareness.* As the President's Cyberspace Policy Review found, people cannot value security without first understanding how much is at risk. Therefore, DHS will enhance its own cybersecurity awareness program and continue to lead the national cybersecurity public awareness campaign aimed at individual users of the Internet, as part of the Administration's National Initiative for Cybersecurity Education. This campaign will empower and support citizens and organizations to use the Internet securely and safely, protecting themselves and the cyber infrastructure.

E. Ensuring Resilience to Disasters

Current Authorities

DHS's role in ensuring resilience to disasters is shaped primarily by the Robert T. Stafford Disaster Relief and Emergency Assistance Act (Stafford Act), the Post Katrina Emergency Management Reform Act (PKEMRA), and other Executive Orders and Congressional mandates. The Homeland Security Act of 2002 identifies as primary mission of the Department the responsibility to act as a focal point regarding natural and manmade crises and emergency planning. Under Title V of the Homeland Security Act, as amended by PKEMRA, the Secretary of Homeland Security, through the FEMA Administrator, is responsible for leading the Nation's efforts to prepare for, protect against, respond to, recover from, and mitigate against the risk of natural disasters, acts of terrorism, and other man-made disasters, including catastrophic incidents. The Stafford Act is the Nation's primary authority for all-hazards emergency management; the FEMA Administrator exercises a variety of authorities under the Stafford Act on behalf of the President and the Secretary of Homeland Security. Homeland Security Presidential Directives 5, 8, and 20 make the Secretary of Homeland Security responsible for domestic incident management and national preparedness, and national continuity operations and activities, respectively; these functions are largely carried out by FEMA. Statutes such as the National Flood Insurance Act of 1968, the Earthquake Hazards Reduction Act of 1977, and the National Dam Safety Program Act vest FEMA with significant hazard mitigation authorities. The Implementing the Recommendations of the 9/11 Commission Act of 2007 codify several of the Department's preparedness grant programs. The Federal Fire Prevention and Control Act of 1974 vests FEMA with a variety of fire prevention, preparedness, and response authorities. Further, the Ports and Waterway Safety Act of 1972, amended by the Port and Tanker Safety Act of 1978, authorizes the USCG to establish requirements for vessels and other port safety controls, to minimize threats to the safety and security of U.S. citizens, facilities, vessels, national assets, and the environment. The Comprehensive Environmental Response, Compensation, and Liability Act, the Superfund Act, and the Oil Pollution Act of 1990 establish broad Federal authority to respond to releases or substantial threats of releases of oil and hazardous substances; these authorities are executed by the U.S. Coast Guard in conjunction with the Environmental Protection Agency.

Overview of the DHS Role

Ensuring domestic resilience to disasters is grounded in the four fundamental elements of emergency management: mitigating hazards, increasing our Nation's preparedness, effectively responding to emergencies, and supporting community recovery. The QHSR also highlighted the overarching importance of resilience to the Nation's ability to withstand and recover from disasters. To that end, DHS will foster an approach to disaster management nationally that is built upon a foundation of proactive engagement at the community level that builds community resilience and supports local emergency management needs.

During domestic disasters, the Department's role, largely executed through FEMA, is principally one of coordinator, working closely with our State, local, tribal, and territorial partners, as well as nongovernmental organizations and the private sector, to enhance preparedness, build and sustain capabilities, and act as an aggregator of resources from across the Federal government. DHS, through FEMA, also has specific direct responsibilities, including disaster response and field coordination, disaster logistics, individual and public assistance programs, as well as the lead coordinating role for national continuity programs. DHS maintains significant first responder and coordination capabilities for disasters in the maritime domain through USCG with its broad Captain of the Port authority and role as Federal Maritime Security Coordinator and Federal On-Scene Coordinator in the coastal zone. USCG provides multi-mission surface, air, and shore assets that take action to save lives, minimize damage, and protect the environment. DHS, through the National Protection and Programs Directorate, also ensures the resilience of critical infrastructure to disasters.

Mitigating Hazards

DHS is uniquely positioned not only to support communities during a disaster, but also enable State, local, regional, tribal, and territorial partners to take steps that will decrease risk and mitigate future hazards before a disaster strikes. DHS works closely with our local and regional partners to identify hazards, assess vulnerabilities, and develop strategies to manage the risks associated with natural and man-made hazards. The Department works to reduce risk to life and property through encouraging land use controls and adoption of building codes, while also applying engineering and planning practices in conjunction with advanced technology tools. A primary area of focus is reducing flood loss and damage, by ensuring that communities across the country have access to affordable flood insurance while also encouraging communities to adopt and enforce floodplain management regulations that mitigate the effects of flooding. DHS also enhances structural resilience through interrelated stewardship and safety responsibilities, particularly in the maritime sector.

Enhancing Preparedness

Increasing preparedness is a key responsibility of DHS. This responsibility includes working collaboratively to increase the preparedness of our State, local, regional, tribal, and territorial partners, as well as nongovernmental organizations, the private sector, and the general public. DHS has responsibility for crafting a national preparedness goal and system and building preparedness capabilities through planning, training, safety and security standards, technical assistance, exercises and credentialing for homeland security partners and stakeholders at all levels of government and industry. The primary vehicle for enhancing preparedness at the State, local, regional, tribal, and territorial level are grant programs—notably the State Homeland Security Grant Program and Urban Areas Security Initiative—which along with other grant programs collectively provide almost $4 billion annually to State, local, regional, tribal, and territorial governments. The Department is also the lead in providing guidance and resources to aid in building preparedness at the local and regional level by encouraging individuals and families, the private sector and community-based organizations to reduce vulnerabilities and improve their capacity to withstand disasters through planning, readiness, and capacity-building activities. To this end, DHS works closely with local and regional officials and first responders encouraging public preparedness activities and awareness campaigns, and works with a number of national networks of community based preparedness teams. Federally-administered training programs—such as FEMA's National Domestic Preparedness Consortium, Emergency Management Institute, and Center for Domestic Preparedness—also play a critical role in developing the knowledge, skills, and abilities of stakeholders in the private sector and at all levels of government. DHS, through USCG, establishes and enforces safety and security regulations on mariners, vessels, and maritime facilities to ensure all-hazard preparedness. Finally, DHS improves catastrophic preparedness through the establishment of shared preparedness and response objectives and planning for responding to extreme events.

Ensuring Effective Disaster Response

DHS, primarily through FEMA, acts as the Federal coordinator during disaster response, supporting State, local, regional, tribal, and territorial governments while working closely with nongovernmental organizations and the private sector to help leverage the resources that they can bring to bear. This coordination ensures that our Nation's emergency response is functioning in a comprehensive, unified manner. To meet disaster response requirements, FEMA maintains Incident Management Assistance Teams, the National Urban Search and Rescue Response System, Mobile Emergency Response Support Detachments, the National Response Coordination Center and a network of Regional Response Coordination Centers, disaster emergency and interoperable communications capabilities, a robust disaster logistics capability, and recovery programs to provide public assistance and individual assistance to affected citizens. DHS, through FEMA, also disseminates emergency alert information during an emergency through the Integrated Public Alert and Warning System (IPAWS) which is designed to provide a multi-faceted dissemination mechanism for alerts beyond traditional audio-only and television warnings. The IPAWS program leverages technological advancements in how messages can be disseminated as well as how, and on what types of devices, they can be received in the event of an emergency. Through USCG, DHS also maintains robust multi-mission first responder assets capable of saving lives, protecting property and the environment, and responding to all-hazards disasters within the maritime domain. USCG, together with the Environmental Protection Agency, coordinates the response to Spills of National Significance under the National Contingency Plan for oil and other hazardous materials spills in navigable waterways.

Supporting Community Recovery

DHS plays a key role in facilitating community recovery following a disaster. Through FEMA's Public Assistance and Individual Assistance programs, DHS is able to support eligible reconstruction projects and provide eligible disaster survivors with financial support as they begin the road to recovery. In conjunction with the Small Business Administration and the Departments of Housing and Urban Development, Agriculture, and other Federal agencies, the Department also provides State, local, tribal, and territorial governments with access to subject matter experts to assist local governments with planning and coordinating the rebuilding efforts. In addition, FEMA serves in a key role to ensure government-wide continuity of operations in the event of a disaster. USCG "first responder" assets quickly become recovery platforms following a maritime disaster and play critical roles in restoring the Maritime Transportation System and the flow of commerce through our ports and waterways. USCG and CBP have substantial responsibilities for facilitating the restoration of trade following a major disruption due to disaster.

The devastating effects of recent disasters have highlighted the need to reform our national approach to long-term recovery. Communities devastated by a disaster, particularly large-scale and catastrophic events such as Hurricane Katrina face complex and difficult challenges, including restoring economic viability, rebuilding infrastructure and public services, and establishing resilience against future hazards. To that end, in September 2009, the President directed DHS and the Department of Housing and Urban Development (HUD) to co-chair an interagency working group to strengthen long-term disaster recovery at the Federal, State, local, tribal, and territorial levels. Following an extensive outreach effort with stakeholders across the country, this effort will result in two documents in 2010: a National Disaster Recovery Framework (NDRF) and a report to the President with specific recommendations to improve the Nation's capacity for effective long-term recovery. The NDRF, a companion document to the

National Response Framework, will outline how community recovery is supported on a national level. The report to the President will recommend improvements to the way in which government at all levels, the private sector, non-profit organizations, communities, and individuals prepare for and recover from a disaster. DHS's efforts, through FEMA, will include a particular focus on enhancing the delivery of recovery support functions for which FEMA is directly responsible, such as funding for public infrastructure rebuilding.

Initiatives and Enhancements

The QHSR and BUR analyses show that DHS's responsibilities in disaster resilience require enhanced planning, management systems, resilience policies, and the promotion of individual, family and community preparedness. Planning for catastrophic disasters must be more coordinated and predicated on nationally agreed-upon, risk-based preparedness standards. FEMA personnel must be developed to further enhance DHS's ability to lead in emergency management. DHS must lead non-governmental sectors in setting infrastructure design standards and get expanded authority to regulate high-risk assets. Finally, new mechanisms are needed to enhance preparedness at the community, family, and individual levels.

Therefore, DHS will undertake the following initiatives and enhancements to enhance catastrophic disaster preparedness, improve DHS' ability to lead in emergency management, explore opportunities with the private sector to "design-in" greater resilience for critical infrastructure, and make individual and family preparedness and critical facility resilience inherent in community preparedness.

- *Enhance catastrophic disaster preparedness.* Of particular importance to DHS is our national preparedness for catastrophic events. National efforts to ensure resilience to these events must focus on improving existing catastrophic preparedness. This requires close collaboration with all partners to establish shared objectives and capability standards at the Federal, State, local, regional, tribal, territorial, nongovernmental, and private sector levels. We must engage and integrate the public as part of the solution to achieving greater overall catastrophic preparedness. Planning assumptions must address risk-based worst case scenarios (maximums of maximums) with resource thresholds that are intended to challenge preparedness at all levels of government. These scenarios will enable planners to seek innovative, non-traditional solutions to catastrophic events. Partnerships in planning for these events will also extend beyond the traditional coalitions, that involve Federal, State, local, regional, tribal, territorial, community planners, the private sector, and nonprofit organizations. Plans will be supported by training, technical assistance and grants, and ultimately be validated through robust exercises designed to overload the system so additional capability shortfalls can be identified and addressed.

- *Improve DHS' ability to lead in emergency management.* To improve overall effectiveness in emergency management, FEMA will create a new strategic approach to developing the agency's current workforce, recruiting and hiring the best talent available and strengthening skill sets across the workforce in support of FEMA's core responsibilities. DHS will create a career path for employees with emergency management responsibilities, including headquarters positions, field deployments, and mobility assignments, and implement both paid and unpaid internship programs to develop future emergency managers. FEMA will implement personnel exchanges between headquarters and regional offices to enhance employee understanding of headquarters and regional perspectives, as well as personnel exchanges between FEMA and State governments through the Intergovernmental Personnel Act. DHS will reassess, refine, and clarify roles and responsibilities for emergency management through the *National Response Framework* revision process, which will help streamline the delivery of effective disaster response. DHS will also promote access to emergency management-related information by homeland security partners and stakeholders, in order to promote a shared understanding of how risks are prioritized and managed and inform resource allocation decisions. Finally, DHS will align FLETC State, local, regional, tribal, and territorial law enforcement with training through FEMA's National Domestic Preparedness Consortium, Emergency Management Institute, and Center for Domestic Preparedness in order to harmonize curriculums and take advantage of complementary learning experiences. DHS will also enhance coordination of existing fellowship programs that receive DHS support to ensure coordination and maximize the effectiveness and utility of those programs.

- *Explore opportunities with the private sector to "design-in" greater resilience for critical infrastructure.* Our efforts to reduce vulnerabilities to critical infrastructure and key resources must include not only physical protection measures but also inherent resilience. It is more efficient and more effective to build in resilience by design than to retrofit for resilience once facilities and networks are developed. To that end, DHS will work with nongovernmental organizations that set infrastructure design standards to establish commonly-agreed standards for critical infrastructure resilience. DHS will build upon the standards adoption authority provided under Title IX of the Implementing the 9/11 Recommendations Act of 2007, and will seek to incorporate design standards for critical infrastructure resilience into Federally-administered insurance and re-insurance programs. DHS will also examine the need to set security requirements at high-risk assets and in high-risk areas as appropriate, and to set standards for security practices in critical infrastructure sectors as necessary. Finally, DHS will seek to obtain information from the private sector with protections preventing such information from unnecessary disclosure, in order to allow DHS to make determinations concerning risk.

- *Make individual and family preparedness and critical facility resilience inherent in community preparedness.* Preparedness and hazard vulnerability reduction must be inherent in communities in the same way that protection and resilience must be built into critical infrastructure by design. DHS will work with its Federal, State, local, tribal, territorial, nongovernmental, and private sector partners to develop new mechanisms for building in preparedness and hazard vulnerability reduction into urban planning, community-provided education, and civic organizations.

F. Complementary Department Responsibilities and Hybrid Capabilities

DHS also performs a number of services and functions that are complementary to its homeland security mission responsibilities, including marine safety, stewardship, and environmental protection and certain categories of law enforcement activities. These services and functions are typically performed with hybrid capabilities—assets and resources capable of performing multiple missions—which are a hallmark of homeland security. For example, the same assets and personnel that patrol our borders, enforce our immigration laws, and respond to major oil spills also enforce safety regulations, assist travelers, and safeguard natural resources. These complementary activities are critical to fulfilling other national interests, and are often intertwined with and mutually supporting of homeland security activities.

IV. Improving Department Management

As noted earlier, the integration of all or part of 22 different Federal departments and agencies into a unified, integrated Department of Homeland Security continues to represent a significant public policy and management challenge. In its seven years of existence, DHS has taken significant steps to create a unified and integrated Department, and the bottom-up review process has provided a unique opportunity to examine and improve the way the Department runs itself.

The DHS Efficiency Review

To unify the Department, the Secretary launched a major initiative to foster a culture of responsibility and fiscal discipline, cut costs, and streamline operations through a series of measures that are expected to lead to significant cost avoidances. Since its launch in March 2009, the DHS Efficiency Review program has implemented nearly two dozen separate initiatives to achieve these aims while also promoting greater accountability, transparency, and customer satisfaction. The Efficiency Review has led to improvements in how the Department manages its resources in several areas, including its physical assets and support of its workforce, as well as the day-to-day expenditures required to do business. As part of the Efficiency Review and through other channels, DHS has also made improvements in how it supports its workforce. An expanded discussion of Efficiency Review initiatives is set forth at Annex C to this report.

A DHS International Engagement Framework

The flow of people and goods around the world and across U.S. borders can advance America's interests, but can also create security challenges that are increasingly borderless and unconventional. Within this environment, DHS has a core responsibility to ensure the safety, security, and resiliency of the United States and the global trade and travel systems upon which our Nation relies.

In order to fulfill its full range of missions, DHS must build on U.S. international partnerships to enhance our ability to identify vulnerabilities and to understand, investigate, and interdict threats at the earliest possible point, ideally before they become manifest, reach our shores, or disrupt the critical networks on which we depend. To that end, DHS will be developing a strategic framework for DHS international engagement to provide common policy objectives and priorities across the Department. The framework will prioritize the Department's engagement, activities, and footprint abroad, and advance DHS's ability to meet future challenges around the world. This international framework will be consistent with the broad range of U.S. Government international priorities and in consultation and coordination with the Department of State and the U.S. Chiefs of Mission in foreign countries.

The DHS international engagement framework will focus on the following areas of emphasis:

- Increased cooperation with international partners to identify, prevent, deter, investigate, and disrupt threats, and manage homeland security risks through dynamic information and knowledge sharing and cooperation in joint operations;

- Enhanced collaboration with international partners to develop norms, standards, and regulatory environments that enhance international security activities relating to homeland security, including aviation security, maritime security, and global supply chain security;

- Enhanced collaboration with international partners in technology development and evaluation for homeland security applications; and

- Increased capacity building, training, and technical assistance in partnership with the Departments of State and Defense to strengthen weak links in the global systems that move people and goods.

Initiatives and Enhancements

The QHSR statute required an assessment of the organizational alignment of the Department with the national homeland security strategy and homeland security missions set forth in the QHSR Report. The BUR included this assessment. The assessment showed that six years since its establishment as a Federal department, there remain critical opportunities to enhance integration across DHS, including operationally by ensuring clear delineation of headquarters and operational components; aligning the multiple regional structures that exist across operational components nationally; strengthening training and career paths through emphasis on mobility and cross-disciplinary experiences; and enhancing management and functional integration. Currently, the Secretary of Homeland Security cannot reorganize DHS in the manner envisioned by the Homeland Security Act, thereby severely limiting her ability to manage the department through a rapidly evolving security environment. Though much progress has been made in adopting a risk management posture and culture across DHS, there remains work to be done in carrying out a national risk assessment and further inculcating risk management principles and priorities throughout all DHS activities. Lastly, the health and resilience of DHS employees must remain an urgent management priority, as should the conversion of contractor to government positions.

At the core of DHS operations are its seven operating components: U.S. Citizenship and Immigration Services (USCIS); the U.S Coast Guard (USCG); U.S. Customs and Border Protection (CBP); the Federal Emergency Management Agency (FEMA); U.S. Immigration and

Customs Enforcement (ICE); U.S. Secret Service (USSS); and the Transportation Security Administration (TSA).

To improve Department management, DHS proposes to restore the Secretary's reorganization authority for DHS headquarters, realign component regional configurations into a single DHS regional structure, improve cross-Departmental management and functional integration, strengthen DHS intelligence and counterintelligence capabilities, enhance the Department's risk management capability, increase coordination within DHS through cross-Departmental training, enhance the DHS workforce through more developed career paths, and increased diversity, especially at senior levels, and reduce reliance on contractors.

- *Seek restoration of the Secretary's reorganization authority for DHS headquarters.* At its founding, DHS was authorized to conduct reorganizations of Department functions upon 60 days notice to Congress, with the exception of USSS and USCG. Over time, Congress has limited that authority to a point where today the Secretary is restricted from using that authority at all. To provide the Secretary with the authority to realign the Department's headquarters to meet new threats and realize greater efficiencies, DHS will request that Congress remove current restrictions on the Department's ability to use its authority under Section 872 of the Homeland Security Act of 2002 with respect to its headquarters.

- *Realign component regional configurations into a single DHS regional structure.* Each of DHS's seven current operating components use a different regional structure for locating offices, allocating resources, and conducting operations and planning across the United States. To streamline operations nationally, increase efficiencies, and enhance cross-training and rotational assignments, DHS will align the seven separate regional structures currently in use by the operating components to a single, nationwide regional structure. DHS is currently examining the best mechanism for harmonizing and integrating its regional structure, including any recommendations regarding legislative authority necessary to effectuate such an alignment.

- *Improve cross-Departmental management, policy, and functional integration.* DHS's business chiefs (e.g. Chief Financial Officer, Chief Information Officer) conduct cross-Department management and oversight as well as perform day-to-day service functions for DHS headquarters directorates and offices. In order to improve cross-Department management, DHS will examine the creation of a Headquarters Services Division within the Management Directorate from the existing service functions of the business chiefs that will provide day-to-day business support functions to DHS headquarters elements. In order to increase cross-Departmental policy development and coordination, DHS will also seek to elevate the position of Assistant Secretary for Policy to an Under Secretary.

    To transform and increase the integration of Departmental management functions, DHS is concentrating on seven specific initiatives: Enterprise Governance; a Balanced Workforce Strategy; Transformation and Systems Consolidation (TASC); Headquarters Consolidation and St. Elizabeth's; Human Resources Information Technology; Data Center Migration; and Homeland Security Presidential Directive 12 Implementation.

These initiatives will help drive transformation to a "One DHS" culture through cohesive horizontal and vertical integration and management of Department-wide initiatives, improve the transparency and functionality of critical management systems, increase cybersecurity of our networks through consolidation of data centers, effectively manage real estate in the National Capital Region, and create common identification procedures within DHS. Full implementation of Homeland Security Presidential Directive 12, including a single DHS identification card and common operating procedures and protocols for employee and contractor access, will ensure a single secure identification credential for all of DHS.

- *Strengthen internal DHS counterintelligence capabilities.* It is imperative for DHS to have an effective and coherent counterintelligence effort. DHS will enhance its counterintelligence capabilities and posture through increased training and reporting, pre-briefing and de-briefing of employees traveling abroad and recurrent vetting programs for contractor personnel. DHS will also develop a cyber counterintelligence capability to complement existing information assurance activities. In addition, DHS will address structural impediments to improving the counterintelligence function within the Department by integrating currently separated counterintelligence activities into a unified counterintelligence program.

- *Enhance the Department's risk management capability.* As the QHSR identified, ultimately homeland security is about effectively managing the risks to the Nation. Employing an integrated risk management framework, DHS will enhance its capability to inform strategies, processes, and decisions to enhance security and to work in a unified manner with its homeland security partners to manage risks. DHS will continue building this framework and invest in the governance, policy, guidance, processes, tools, training, and accountability necessary to manage risk. DHS will also continue to work to evaluate all hazards risks to the Nation, identify improved strategies for managing risks, and measure performance in terms of risk reduction.

- *Strengthen coordination within DHS through cross-Departmental training and career paths.* DHS's most valuable resource is its people. Thus, any effort to achieve a unified DHS must focus on the men and women who work at DHS. DHS will strengthen Department unity by developing DHS career paths that provide mobility within the Department and span headquarters and operational components. DHS will also increase the number of DHS component personnel on rotation in headquarters directorates and offices, and the number of DHS headquarters personnel on rotation in components. As part of interagency national security and homeland security professional development, DHS will also explore interagency and intergovernmental rotational assignments with Federal, State, local, tribal, and territorial partners.

- *Enhance the DHS workforce.* The Department's health, wellness, and resilience programs are critical to employee retention and performance. DHS has created programs such as the DHS Together Employee Initiative and the Organizational Resilience Initiative to ensure that Department employees have the tools and resources to manage the stresses inherent in these occupations. DHS also plans to implement Workplace

Wellness programs, including employee resilience training, to address the needs of the Department's diverse workforce. DHS will create a standardized, metrics-driven health program that supports the unique needs of our operational workforce, and frontline medical programs that support operational missions staffed and supported with appropriate training and equipment. DHS will also expand TSA's Idea Factory across the Department in order to harness the insights and innovations of the DHS workforce.

In addition, the Department will pursue greater diversity in its workforce, especially at senior levels. Given our critical homeland security mission, DHS must focus on the diversity of its workforce to reflect the people it serves. The Secretary recently appointed a senior-level steering committee, chaired by the Deputy Secretary, to direct a multi-year effort to promote diversity. DHS has initiated a coordinated employee recruitment initiative to improve diversity of applicant pools. This approach will emphasize targeted recruitment to increase the number of women, minorities, and veterans applying to work throughout DHS and enterprise recruitment efforts for Senior Executive Service positions. We will also deploy a Department-wide exit survey to provide more reliable information about employee attrition and to understand how this impacts diversity in the Department.

- *Balance the DHS workforce by ensuring strong federal control of all DHS work and reducing reliance on contractors.* DHS is strongly committed to a full re-examination of its workforce needs and its current reliance on contractors. In 2009, all DHS directorates, components, and offices were directed to examine current contracts and develop initial contractor conversion plans. Over the past year, the Department has been actively converting contractor positions to government positions. DHS will continue to build on these efforts at an even more aggressive pace to put in place the appropriate federal workforce required to oversee and carry out its mission responsibilities.

V. Increasing Accountability

To enhance mission performance and improve Departmental management, DHS must increase accountability across the organization. While accountability cuts across all aspects of the organization's operations, our initial focus will be to maximize the performance and resource data we collect to inform strategic and risk-informed decision-making.

Data and Performance Management

Seven years of Departmental operation have led to significant gains in cross-Departmental relationships, particularly at the operational level, but significant differences still remain. These differences can hinder effective decision-making and accountability.

For many of its early years, DHS did not have mature strategic planning, resource allocation, execution oversight, and reporting processes. The QHSR was a major milestone in the Department's strategic planning process; it has demonstrated both internally and externally the value of strategic planning and that strategic planning is possible within the homeland security mission space. The last few years have seen increased maturity in resource allocation and execution oversight, particularly acquisition oversight. The Department has also systematically improved its financial management by building a strong internal controls process and focusing attention on the elimination of material weaknesses in financial audits.

Congressional Accountability

As the 9/11 Commission noted in its report, "Congress needs to establish for the Department of Homeland Security the kind of clear authority and responsibility that exist to enable ... the Defense Department to deal with threats to national security." Both the House and Senate Appropriations committees have consolidated all DHS jurisdiction into a single subcommittee within each chamber. Each chamber has also designated one authorization committee with primary oversight over DHS. However, DHS has had 86 committees and subcommittees exercising jurisdiction over the Department in each session of Congress since 2003. As a result, to date in the 111th Congress, DHS has provided testimony in more than 200 hearings from more than 280 Department witnesses. Over the past year, DHS provided approximately 5,227 Congressional briefings, formal and informal. A diagram of Congressional oversight of DHS in the 110th Congress is attached as Annex F. Streamlining Congressional oversight of DHS would allow the Department to focus its time and resources much more effectively on its critical missions, while preserving a full degree of accountability to Congress.

Initiatives and Enhancements

The QHSR established a foundation that will permit more effective and targeted analysis of DHS mission effectiveness. The QHSR legislation also required a review and assessment of the effectiveness of the mechanisms of the Department for executing the process of turning the requirements developed in the QHSR into an acquisition strategy and expenditure plan within the Department. DHS conducted this analysis. DHS does not have a common analytic framework like that of the Department of Defense, which facilitates cross-Departmental planning and capability development. DHS will establish a common framework to effectively identify and assess alternatives and support decision-making at all levels. Additionally, the performance metrics that flow from department-wide analysis must be a priority for further development and refinement, both at the strategic and program levels. Lastly, though the Cost Analysis Division is an important step in the department's improved acquisition oversight, there remains a vital need for independent cost assessments of major programs. These initiatives are intended to improve the effectiveness of the mechanisms of the Department for executing the process of turning the requirements developed in the QHSR into an acquisition strategy and expenditure plan within the Department.

- *Increase Analytic Capability and Capacity.* Increasing the Department's analytic capability and capacity will help Department leadership better understand the implications of major decisions and the costs of alternative actions. DHS will enhance its strategic planning processes, resource allocation processes, risk analyses, net assessments, modeling capabilities, statistical analyses, and data collection in order to effectively project capability and capacity requirements for DHS missions and functions. DHS will take steps to develop common analytic frameworks and assumptions for use in cross-Departmental analysis, similar to the Department of Defense's Analytic Agenda initiative. DHS will also reform its budget account structure to increase its ability to compare like costs across components and offices. As these reforms take shape, DHS will seek Congressional approval to conform its appropriations structure to this reformed account structure.

- *Improve Performance Measurement and Accountability.* Along with increased analytic capability and capacity, the Department must increase the quality of its performance measures and link those measures to the mission outcomes articulated in the QHSR Report. DHS has been actively working with the Government Accountability Office to address shortfalls in its current program performance measures, and the QHSR strategic framework provides the foundation upon which to base new strategic outcomes and measures. To that end, the Department will adjust its program-level performance measures, and introduce new strategic-level performance measures for cross-Departmental missions and functions. DHS will also expand program evaluation during and after program execution.

- *Strengthen Acquisition Oversight.* DHS has made significant improvements in acquisition oversight in the last two years; however, the Department needs to continue to strengthen this process. Numerous audits conducted by the Government Accountability Office and DHS Inspector General have highlighted significant program cost growth and the inadequacy of the cost estimating process across DHS. DHS has established a Cost Analysis Division (CAD) in the Office of the Chief Procurement Officer. Currently, the CAD is responsible for validating Program Life Cycle Cost Estimates. As a next step in its acquisition oversight process, DHS proposes to increase CAD's capability to provide independent cost estimates of major programs at major milestone points. This capability will ensure program cost estimates are reasonable reflections of the program's requirements and can withstand the scrutiny of external reviews and audits. Reliable and credible independent cost estimates will increase the Department's capability for informed investment decision making, budget formulation, progress measurement and accountability. Rigorous analyses of operational requirements, technology alternatives and disciplined testing and evaluation of technology acquisitions will be instituted to ensure investments yield intended mission improvements.

VI. Conclusion

The Quadrennial Homeland Security Review, consistent with the *National Security Strategy*, was the first step in setting forth the strategic foundation to guide the activities of the homeland security enterprise toward a common end. This BUR report represents a second, DHS-focused step, and comprehensive effort to align the Department's programmatic activities and organizational structure with the mission sets and goals identified in the QHSR. The BUR serves as a road map for areas where additional emphasis, investment, and effort are needed to strengthen mission performance, improve Departmental operations and management and increase accountability for the resources entrusted to DHS.

The final step will be to execute the BUR. The BUR and QHSR will be implemented in the DHS FY 2012-2016 Future Years Homeland Security Program to Congress, which will propose specific programmatic adjustments based on the BUR recommendations. DHS will also undertake, in coordination with appropriate interagency partners, additional efforts in support of the QHSR, including the development of requirements for intelligence, science and technology, support to civil authorities, and other elements described in this report. Together, the QHSR, the bottom-up review, and the budget proposals will serve as vital steps in maturing DHS into a truly strategy-driven organization.

As noted in the QHSR, the over-arching message is clear: this is a strong and resilient Nation, but one that must consistently adjust to an ever-changing threat environment. There are many critical roles to play—at DHS, across the Federal government, in Congress, throughout State, local, tribal, and territorial governments, within the private sector, and by families and in communities across the Nation. Through the commitment of each, we will secure the homeland for all.

Annex A
DHS Component Composition

The Department of Homeland Security has a dynamic and complex mission and continually evaluates its force needs to optimally secure the homeland. The current composition of DHS forces is provided below. The QHSR and BUR results will be implemented in the FY 2012-2016 Future Years Homeland Security Program (FYHSP), which may drive additional changes. (Employee numbers are rounded)

Transportation Security Administration (TSA):

Headquarters and Supporting Resources
      Operations Coordination Center
      HQ Intelligence Office and Field Intelligence Officers
      TSA Representation (19 countries)
      Vetting and Credentialing Centers (primary and Back-up) (2)
      Federal Flight Deck Officer Training Facilities (2)
Airport Passenger and Baggage Screening Operations (450 Airports)
      Transportation Security Officers (45,000)
      Behavior Detection Officers (3,000)
      Bomb Appraisal Officers (400)
      Canine Teams (165 Proprietary; 640 Agreements)
In-Flight Air Security
      Federal Air Marshal Service
Surface and Multi-Modal Security
      Multi-Modal Visible Intermodal Prevention and Response Teams (VIPR) (10)
      Surface Transportation VIPR Teams (15)

U.S. Customs and Border Protection (CBP):

Headquarters and Supporting Resources
Air, Land, and Sea Ports of Entry (327)
      Process Passengers and Pedestrians
      CBP Officers (21,000)
      Agricultural Specialists (2,000)
Border Security between Ports of Entry
      20 Border Patrol sectors with 139 stations
      Border Patrol Agents (20,000)
Air and Marine Operations (46 Air Units and 67 Marine Units)
      Air Interdiction Agents (800)
      Marine Interdiction Agents (350)
      Assets
        Aircraft (290)
        Marine Vessels (235)

U.S. Citizenship and Immigration Service (USCIS):

Headquarters and Supporting Resources
Immigration Benefits Processing
       District Offices providing adjudication of applications and petitions (26)
       Service Center Operations (4)
       Asylum Offices providing adjudication of asylum applications (8 domestic offices)
       Refugee Offices providing adjudication of refugee applications (over 70 global offices)
       International Operations (30 field offices)
       Application Support Centers (129)
Citizen Outreach
       Information Call Centers
Fraud Detection and National Security
       Immigration Officers vetting of fraud and national security concerns (650)

U.S. Immigration and Customs Enforcement (ICE):

Headquarters and Supporting Resources
Office of Investigations
       Special Agents in Charge Offices (SACS) (26)
       Criminal Investigators (6,600)
Office of Detention and Removal Operations
       Field Office Directors (27)
       Detention Officers (7,200)
       Detention Beds (33,000)
Office of the Principal Legal Advisor
       Division Chiefs (13)
       Chief Counsel (26)
       Attorneys (851)
Office of International Affairs
       Attaché/Assistant Attaché Offices (63)
       Special Agents (337)
       Deportation Liaison Officers/ Detention & Deportation Officer (1801) (18)
       Intelligence Research Specialists/Analysts (4)
       Foreign Service Nationals (118)
Office of Professional Responsibility
       Special Agents in Charge Offices (5)
       Office locations nationwide (24)
       Special Agents (323)
Office of Intelligence
       Field Intelligence Directors (26)
       Special Agents (66)

U.S. Secret Service (USSS):

Headquarters and Supporting Resources
      Headquarters Divisions/Offices (30)
      Administrative, Professional, and Technical Personnel (1,800)
Protection and Investigations
      Permanent Protective Details (8)
      Special Agents (3,500)
      Uniformed Division Officers (1,400)
      Domestic Offices (116)
      Foreign Offices (20)

Federal Emergency Management Agency (FEMA):

Workforce
      A blended workforce of 16,590 with 4,200 permanent, 3,390 temporary and 9,000
      reserve employees
Headquarters and Supporting Resources (1,988: 1,539 perm; 382 temp; 67 reserve)
      Mount Weather Emergency Operations Center (837: 669 perm; 166 temp; 2 reserve)
National Emergency Training Center (NETC) training facility (243), includes:
      Emergency Management Institute (EMI) (58 perm; 15 temp; 9 reserve)
      National Fire Academy (NFA) (110 perm; 1 temp)
      Center for Domestic Preparedness (CDP) training facility (50 perm)
Regional offices (10) and Area Offices (3)
      Region 1 (100 perm; 17 temp; 570 reserve)
      Region 2 (107 perm; 10 temp; 608 reserve)
      Region 3 (101 perm; 14 temp; 519 reserve)
      Region 4 (156 perm; 91 temp; 1311 reserve)
      Region 5 (126 perm; 17 temp; 439 reserve)
      Region 6 (126 perm; 85 temp; 912 reserve)
      Region 7 (97 perm; 58 temp; 446 reserve)
      Region 8 (89 perm; 20 temp; 433 reserve)
      Region 9 (126 perm; 22 temp; 473 reserve)
      Region 10 (97 perm; 15 temp; 585 perm)
      Texas Transitional Recovery Office (1 temp)
      Louisiana Transitional Recovery Office (1 perm; 485 temp)
      Mississippi Transitional Recovery Office (276 temp)
Disaster Reservists (9,000)
Disaster Support Resources
      National Response Coordination Center (NRCC) (1)
      Regional Response Coordination Centers (RRCC) (10)
      Federal Coordinating Officers (FCO) (1 perm; 37 temp)
      National Incident Management Assistance Teams (IMAT) (2)
      Regional Incident Management Assistance Teams (IMAT) (4)
      Mobile Emergency Response Support (MERS) Detachments (6), each comprised of:
            MERS Operations Centers (MOC)

Incident Response Vehicle (IRV) capability
Mobile Emergency Operations Vehicle (MEOV) capability
Forward Communications Vehicle (FCV) capability
Logistics Distribution Centers (8)
Mobile Disaster Recovery Centers (MDRC) (60)

U.S. Coast Guard (USCG):

Workforce
A blended work force with 50,720 active duty and reserve military members, 7,773 civilians, and over 30,000 volunteer members of the Auxiliary.

Support Commands
Coast Guard Headquarters, 2 Area Commands, 9 District Offices, 6 Logistics and Service Centers

Training Centers
6 Major Training Centers: Accession programs for cadets, officer candidates and new recruits and specialized training for Coast Guard job performance.

Shore-Based Multi-Mission Forces
35 Sector Commands with broad maritime safety and security authorities
945 air and marine stations throughout the United States with 1,850 small boats.

Deployable Forces
1 Maritime Security Response Team, 12 Maritime Safety and Security Teams, 8 Port Security Units, 17 Law Enforcement Detachments, 3 Strike Teams

Air and Maritime Fleet
43 Major Cutters, 30 Buoy Tenders, 121 Patrol Boats, 9 Domestic Icebreakers, 3 Polar Icebreakers.
143 Rotary Wing Aircraft, 56 Fixed Wing Aircraft

Annex B
A Day in the Life of the Department of Homeland Security

The Department of Homeland Security uses many tools and areas of expertise to accomplish our goal of securing the homeland. On any given day, we perform a variety of different tasks and functions to make America safer and our citizens more secure. Although our responsibilities are varied, we are united in a common purpose - 24 hours a day, 7 days a week. Below is a sampling of what the men and women of DHS do in a typical day. (All numbers are approximate averages.)

Transportation Security Administration will:
- Screen 2 million passengers and their 1.8 million pieces of checked baggage before they board commercial aircraft
- Intercept 2,000 prohibited items from people and carry-on baggage including 1,200 knives, blades or other sharp objects and 2 firearms
- Operate the National Explosives Detection Canine Team Program, which has 705 explosive detection canine teams deployed across the country
- Deploy thousands of Federal Air Marshals to protect flights in the United States and around the world
- Oversee screening of approximately seven million pounds per day of air cargo on domestic planes
- Conduct 4-5 Visible Intermodal Protection and Reponses operations per day in passenger rail and mass transit systems somewhere in the United States

U.S. Customs and Border Protection will:
- Process over 1 million passengers and pedestrians
- Inspect nearly 60,000 truck, rail and sea containers
- Process $88 million in fees, duties and tariffs
- Make 2,200 apprehensions between ports for illegal entry
- Seize 6,600 pounds of narcotics
- Seize 4,300 prohibited agricultural items
- Make 5,400 pre-departure seizures of prohibited agricultural items

U.S. Citizenship and Immigration Services will:
- Naturalize 2,900 new immigrants
- Conduct 135,000 national security background checks
- Process 27,400 applications for immigrant benefits
- Issue 7,200 permanent resident cards (green cards)
- Capture 8,700 sets of fingerprints at 130 Application Support Centers
- Welcome 3,200 new citizens and 3,300 new permanent residents
- Adjudicate nearly 200 refugee applications from around the world
- Grant asylum to 40 individuals already in the United States

U.S. Immigration and Customs Enforcement will:
- Make 63 administrative arrests and 89 criminal arrests
- Make 11 currency seizures totaling $1.1 million

- Participate in 26 drug seizures each day, totaling 7,200 lbs. of marijuana, 7 lbs. of heroin, and 960 lbs. of cocaine
- ICE attorneys litigate 1,500 cases in immigration court and obtain 740 final orders of removal; 90 of those final orders of removal are for criminal aliens
- Screen 3,800 VISA applications
- House 29,800 illegal aliens in facilities nationwide

United States Secret Service will:
- Protect dozens of high profile government officials including the President, the Vice President, visiting heads of state, and former Presidents
- Seize $319,000 in counterfeit currency and suppress a counterfeit operation
- Open 30 new financial crimes and counterfeit investigations and conduct 26 computer forensic examinations
- Seize $300,000 in assets
- Arrest 25 individuals
- Conduct 8 public education seminars on counterfeit recognition and financial fraud schemes

Federal Emergency Management Agency will:
- Obligate $39 million for disaster response, recovery, and mitigation activities
- Help save $2.7 million in damages from flooding across the country through FEMA's Flood Plain Management
- Help protect an additional 104 homes from the devastating effects of flooding through flood insurance policies issued by the National Flood Insurance Program
- Provide $181,000 for Fire Management Assistance grants, which aid state and local efforts in the suppression of wildfires
- Provide 11,300 publications through FEMA's U.S. Fire Administration to educate citizens about how to stay safe from fire and help America's fire service to safely respond to fires and other emergency incidents
- Arrange for translation services for disaster victims in up to 173 different languages through the National Processing Service Centers in Maryland, Puerto Rico, Texas and Virginia

United States Coast Guard will:
- Save 13 lives, respond to 64 search and rescue cases and prevent loss of $260,000 in property damage
- Seize or remove 1,100 pounds of illegal drugs, with a street value of $19 million
- Interdict 10 migrants attempting to illegally enter the United States via maritime routes
- Conduct 135 armed waterborne patrols projecting presence near maritime critical infrastructure and key resources
- Conduct 57 inspections of U.S. Flagged Vessels and safety exams on commercial fishing vessels
- Conduct 67 container inspections, and investigate and respond to 10 pollution incidents
- Issue 200 credentials to qualified merchant mariners to ensure the safety, security and efficiency of the maritime supply chain

- Perform 47 safety, security and environmental protection inspections at maritime facilities
- Ensure compliance with U.S. and foreign ships with international and U.S. shipboard air emission standards by conducting 32 exams
- Manage 3,500 commercial vessel transits through the Marine Transportation System to facilitate the safe and efficient movement of goods and people
- Provide reliable visual aids to navigation throughout the United States and its territories
- Conduct 14 fisheries boardings to ensure compliance with fisheries and marine protected species regulations
- Provide forces and capabilities to the Department of Defense to carry out U.S. national security objectives

National Protection and Programs Directorate will:
- Protect U.S. information systems through the United States Computer Emergency Readiness Team (US-CERT) by monitoring Federal Executive Branch civilian networks to identify emerging threats, ongoing trends, and intrusions; US-CERT detects and responds to an average of 64 incidents and 3,750 alert events daily
- Disrupt potential terrorist planning activities by conducting 5 Buffer Zone Protection assessments with local law enforcement at critical infrastructure and key resources in every sector across the Nation
- Analyze biometrics data on 100,000 foreign visitors and compare to the Federal watch list of 3.2 million known or suspected terrorists, criminals and immigration violators
- Identify 40 criminal migrants illegally attempting to enter the United States from the sea with biometric data and, through a partnership with the FBI, provide that information to state and local law enforcement agencies
- Use computer modeling and risk analysis to support critical decisions across the Department and to help the Nation prevent, protect, respond, and recover from all hazards
- Prevent 2,100 prohibited items from entering Federal facilities

Science and Technology Directorate will:
- Lead 200 projects to provide solutions to protect us from chemical, biological, and explosive attacks, provide security for our borders and shores, protect key parts of our infrastructure, and mitigate the effects of natural disasters.
- Assess 22 technology companies for product applicability to first responder customers, develop standards for first responder technologies to ensure high quality transitions, and provide test and evaluation services for DHS.

Office of Operations Coordination and Planning (OPS) will:
- Integrate department and interagency strategic level planning and operations coordination across the spectrum of prevent, protect, respond and recover
- Provide DHS with a joint operations coordination and planning capability at the strategic level to support internal DHS operational decision-making and Department leadership and participation in interagency operations
- Provide situational awareness and a common operating picture for the entire Federal government, and for State, local, and tribal governments as appropriate, in the event of a natural disaster, act of terrorism, or other man-made disaster

- Ensure that critical terrorism and disaster-related information reaches government decision-makers

Management Directorate will:
- Hire and process 100 new employees through its human capital office
- Obligate $142 million through its finance office
- Issue 300 contracts through its procurement operations

Office of Intelligence and Analysis will:
- Review all-source intelligence information and produce analysis to distribute to Federal, State, local, tribal, territorial, and private sector partners regarding current and developing threats and vulnerabilities, as well as providing recommendations for potential protective measures

Domestic Nuclear Detection Office will:
- Provide radiation detection equipment to U.S. Customs and Border Protection to scan 70,000 cargo containers for radiological/nuclear material
- Train 12 State and local law enforcement officials on how to use preventive radiological/nuclear detection equipment

Federal Law Enforcement Training Center will:
- Train 3,500 Federal officers and agents from more than 80 different Federal agencies, as well as state, local, tribal and international officers and agents, in one or more of the 400 basic and advanced training programs available

Office of Health Affairs will:
- Retrieve samples from hundreds of BioWatch collectors that have been testing the air in our major metropolitan areas for evidence of biological pathogens
- Screen 350 sources of information from across multiple agencies and venues and assess them for significance and early recognition of a potential bio-event of national significance through the 24 hour watch of the National Biosurveillance Integration Center

Office of Policy will:
- Develop DHS-wide policies, programs, and planning to promote and ensure quality, consistency, and integration across all homeland security missions
- Provide thought leadership and analysis to the Secretary and other Departmental leaders to facilitate decision-making
- Represent the consolidated DHS position at White House interagency policy committee meetings
- Develop and articulate the long-term strategic view of the Department and translate the Secretary's strategic priorities into capstone planning products that drive increased operational effectiveness through integration, prioritization, and resource allocation
- Lead departmental international engagement
- Serve as a single point of contact for experts in academia, the private sector, and other external stakeholders to allow for streamlined policy development and management across the Department

Annex C
The DHS Efficiency Review

The DHS Efficiency Review has focused on improvements regarding physical assets, workforce support, and day-to-day operations. A summary of Efficiency Review and related initiatives is set forth below.

Physical Assets

Strategic refinements in how DHS manages its physical assets have led to savings and improvements. For example, by using excess information technology equipment instead of buying new equipment, DHS has, to date, avoided costs of nearly $3.9 million.

In the area of fleet management, DHS components are making great strides towards increasing the percentage of hybrids and alternative-fuel vehicles in their fleets. Components are also taking steps to encourage the use of alternative fuel instead of petroleum whenever possible.

Initiatives in this area include:

- Implementing an electronic tracking tool for fleet usage data to identify opportunities for alternative fuel usage; heighten vigilance for fraud, waste or abuse; and optimize fleet management;

- Initiating acquisition/leasing of hybrid vehicles for administrative use and alternative-fuel vehicles in cases where hybrids are not feasible;

- Implementing energy efficiencies in all facility management projects; and

- Utilizing wherever possible refurbished IT equipment (computers and mobile devices) and redeploying the current inventory throughout DHS.

Workforce Support

Supporting our workforce by giving them the tools and training they need is good business, and it translates into a more productive and efficient workforce.

Efficiency Review and other initiatives in this area include:

- Identifying and implementing Department-wide strategies to develop and retain our talented workforce, such as providing leadership training to emerging leaders;

- Developing cross-component training opportunities for employees;

- Establishing *Idea Factory* across the Department to encourage all DHS employees to contribute and rate ideas for improved operations;

- Establishing an employee resilience program to help identify and reduce sources of extreme job stress and promote employee wellness;

- Working aggressively to reduce the Department's reliance on contractors and contract services, in turn strengthening our Federal workforce;

- Standardizing content for new-employee orientation and mandatory annual training modules DHS-wide; and

- Focusing on achieving greater diversity in the leadership ranks of the Department.

<u>Day-to-Day Operations</u>

Changing the way the Department allocates resources, from acquiring office supplies to renting facilities, has allowed DHS to significantly reduce those costs. To date, DHS has avoided over $35 million in costs through improved travel and conference planning. In addition, DHS expects to avoid costs of $2.1 million in fiscal year 2010 by consolidating subscriptions for several publications, as well as $138 million in software licensing and maintenance costs over the next six years.

Initiatives in this area include:

- Consolidating subscriptions to professional publications and newspapers and reducing the number of hard copies received by providing online access whenever possible;

- Maximizing the use of government office space for meetings and conferences in place of renting facilities;

- Minimizing the physical printing and distribution of reports and documents that can be sent electronically or posted online;

- Leveraging buying power to acquire software licenses for Department-wide usage;

- Eliminating non-mission critical travel and maximizing use of conference calls and web-based training and meetings;

- Increasing usage of DHS-wide blanket purchase agreements for office supplies; and

- Converting printers, fax machines, copiers, and scanners into all-in-one machines as replacements are needed.

In addition, DHS employees submitted thousands of suggestions in response to the President's SAVE award campaign. Many of these suggestions will be incorporated into the Efficiency Review initiatives in the coming year.

Annex D
Alignment of Major DHS Programs to Homeland Security Missions

In addition to developing the initiatives discussed in the main text of this document, the bottom-up review also conducted a detailed examination of DHS activities and the alignment of these activities to the QHSR mission areas and other complementary Departmental responsibilities for which DHS develops hybrid capabilities. This will facilitate a detailed evaluation of what DHS does within each mission area and identify gaps and overlaps within and across mission areas. This work is also building a foundation for a unified programmatic structure and strategic architecture. This work is ongoing. To provide a view of preliminary alignment, a high-level summary of selected major categories from DHS's existing program structure is shown below. Also shown is a preliminary alignment of DHS's major investments with each mission. Note that while many of these programs and investments cut across multiple mission areas, for display purposes only one alignment is shown.

Preventing Terrorism and Enhancing Security:
- Major FYHSP Programmatic Activity:
  - Aviation Security (TSA)
  - Surface Transportation Security (TSA)
  - Federal Air Marshal Service (TSA)
  - Transportation Threat Assessment and Credentialing (TTAC) (TSA)
  - Domestic Protectees (USSS)
  - Protective Intelligence (USSS)
  - Campaign Protection (USSS)
  - Foreign Protectees and Foreign Missions (USSS)
  - Infrastructure Protection (USSS)
  - Infrastructure Protection (NPPD)
  - Federal Protective Service (NPPD)
  - Domestic Nuclear Detection (DNDO)
  - Medical and Biodefense (OHA)
  - Chemical and Biological Research and Development (S&T)
  - Radiological and Nuclear Research and Development (S&T)
  - Ports, Waterways and Coastal Security (USCG)
- Major Acquisitions and Investments:
  - Electronic Baggage Screening Program (TSA)
  - Passenger Screening Program (TSA)
  - Secure Flight (TSA)
  - Transportation Worker Identification Credentialing (TSA)
  - Advance Spectroscopy Portals (DNDO)
  - Cargo Advanced Automated Radiography System (DNDO)
  - Infrastructure Information Collection and Visualization (NPPD)

Securing and Managing our Borders:
- Major FYHSP Programmatic Activity:
  - Border Security and Control between Ports of Entry (CBP)
  - Border Security Inspections and Trade Facilitation at Ports of Entry (CBP)

- o Border Security Fencing, Infrastructure, and Technology (CBP)
- o Air and Marine (CBP)
- o Automation Modernization (CBP)
- o Drug Interdiction (USCG)
- o Migrant Interdiction (USCG)
- o US-VISIT (NPPD)
- o Border and Maritime Security Research and Development (S&T)
- Major Acquisitions and Investments:
  - o Strategic Air and Marine Plan (CBP)
  - o Secure Border Initiative Net (CBP)
  - o Border Patrol Facilities (CBP)
  - o Non-Intrusive Inspection Systems Program (CBP)
  - o Traveler Enforcement Compliance System Modernization (CBP)
  - o Secure Border Initiative Tactical Infrastructure (CBP)
  - o EWP Tactical Communications (CBP)
  - o License Plate Reader (CBP)
  - o Automated Commercial Environment / International Trade Data System (CBP)
  - o Electronic System for Travel Authorization (CBP)
  - o Secure Freight Initiative (CBP)
  - o Advance Passenger Information System (CBP)
  - o Western Hemisphere Travel Initiative (CBP)
  - o Automated Targeting System (CBP)
  - o Offshore Patrol Cutter (USCG)
  - o National Security Cutter (USCG)
  - o HC-130 Conversion/Sustainment Project (USCG)
  - o HH-65 Conversion/Sustainment Project (USCG)
  - o HC-144A Maritime Patrol Aircraft (USCG)
  - o Medium Endurance Cutter Sustainment (USCG)
  - o Fast Response Cutter - B class (USCG)
  - o Nationwide Automation Identification System (USCG)
  - o HH-60 Conversion/Sustainment Project (USCG)
  - o Unmanned Aircraft Systems (USCG)
  - o Patrol Boat Sustainment (USCG)
  - o HC-130J Fleet Introduction (USCG)
  - o Response Boat – Medium (USCG)
  - o United States Visitor and Immigrant Status Indicator Technology (NPPD)
  - o ATLAS (ICE)

Enforcing and Administering our Immigration Laws:
- Major FYHSP Programmatic Activity:
  - o Adjudication Services (USCIS)
  - o Information and Customer Service (USCIS)
  - o Citizenship (USCIS)
  - o Immigration Status Verification (USCIS)
  - o Immigration Security and Integrity (USCIS)
  - o Investigations (ICE)

- o Detention and Removal Operations (ICE)
- o Automation Modernization (ICE)
- o International Affairs (ICE)
- o Migrant Interdiction (USCG)
- Major Acquisitions and Investments:
  - o Transformation (USCIS)
  - o Integrated Document Production (USCIS)
  - o Verification Information System / Employment Eligibility Verification (USCIS)
  - o Detention and Removal Modernization (ICE)

Safeguarding and Securing Cyberspace:
- Major FYHSP Programmatic Activity:
  - o Cyber Security and Communications (NPPD)
- Major Acquisitions and Investments:
  - o Homeland Security Information Network (AO)
  - o Homeland Secure Data Network (DHS)
  - o National Cybersecurity and Protection System (NPPD)
  - o Information Systems Security (NPPD)

Ensuring Resilience to Disasters:
- Major FYHSP Programmatic Activity:
  - o Mitigation (FEMA)
  - o National Preparedness (FEMA)
  - o Disaster Operations (FEMA)
  - o Disaster Assistance (FEMA)
  - o Logistics Management (FEMA)
  - o U.S. Fire Administration (FEMA)
  - o National Continuity Programs (FEMA)
  - o Search and Rescue (USCG)
- Major Acquisitions and Investments:
  - o BioWatch Gen-3 (OHA)
  - o National Bio and Agro-Defense Facility (S&T)
  - o National Biodefense Analysis and Countermeasures Center Facility (S&T)
  - o Risk Mapping, Analysis and Planning (FEMA)
  - o Housing Inspection Services (FEMA)
  - o Risk Mapping, Analysis and Planning IT (FEMA)
  - o Total Asset Visibility (FEMA)
  - o C4ISR – COP (USCG)
  - o Interagency Operations Centers (Command 21) (USCG)
  - o Rescue 21 (USCG)

Complementary Departmental Responsibilities and Hybrid Capabilities

As noted above, DHS also performs a number of services and functions that are complementary to its homeland security mission responsibilities, including marine safety, stewardship, and environmental protection and certain categories of law enforcement activities. These services and functions are typically performed with hybrid capabilities—assets and resources capable of performing multiple missions—which are a hallmark of homeland security. For example, the same assets and personnel that patrol our borders, enforce our immigration laws, and respond to major oil spills also enforce safety regulations, assist travelers, and safeguard natural resources. These complementary activities are critical to fulfilling other national interests, and are often intertwined with and mutually supporting of homeland security activities. Some of these activities include the following:

- o Major FYHSP Programmatic Activity:
  - o Marine Environmental Protection (USCG)
  - o Marine Safety (USCG)
  - o Other Law Enforcement (USCG)
  - o Living Marine Resources (USCG)
  - o Search and Rescue (USCG)
  - o Defense Readiness (USCG)
  - o Waterways Management: Aids to Navigation (USCG)
  - o Waterways Management: Ice Operations (USCG)
  - o Financial Investigations (USSS)

As the Department continues to evaluate its inventory of activities, it will gain increased insight into those Departmental activities that are complementary to its homeland security mission responsibilities but remain vital and continue to be performed most effectively and efficiently by DHS. This additional breakout will be provided in the President's FY 2012 Budget and the accompanying FY 2012-2016 Future Years Homeland Security Program.

Annex E
Sector-Specific Agencies
(Source: *National Infrastructure Protection Plan*)

Sector-Specific Agency	Critical Infrastructure and Key Resources Sector
Department of Agriculture (a) Department of Health and Human Services(b)	Agriculture and Food
Department of Defense (c)	Defense and Industrial Base
Department of Energy	Energy (d)
Department of Health and Human Services	Healthcare and Public Health
Department of the Interior	National Monuments and Icons
Department of the Treasury	Banking and Finance
Environmental Protection Agency	Water (e)
Department of Homeland Security Office of Infrastructure Protection	Chemical Commercial Facilities Critical Manufacturing Dams Emergency Services Nuclear Reactors, Materials, and Waste Government Facilities (g)
Office of Cybersecurity and Communications	Information Technology Communications
Transportation Security Administration	Postal and Shipping
Transportation Security Administration United States Coast Guard (f)	Transportation Systems (h)

a The Department of Agriculture is respons ble for agriculture and food (meat, poultry, and egg products).
b The Department of Health and Human Services is responsible for food other than meat, poultry, and egg products.
c Nothing in this plan impairs or otherwise affects the authority of the Secretary of Defense over the Department of Defense (DOD), including the chain of command for military forces from the President as Commander in Chief, to the Secretary of Defense, to the commander of military forces, or military command and control procedures.
d The Energy Sector includes the production, refining, storage, and distr bution of oil, gas, and electric power, except for commercial nuclear power facilities.
e The Water Sector includes drinking water and wastewater systems.
f The U.S. Coast Guard is the SSA for the maritime transportation mode.
g The Department of Education is the SSA for the Education Facilities Subsector of the Government Facilities Sector.
h As stated in HSPD-7, the Department of Transportation and the Department of Homeland Security will collaborate on all matters relating to transportation security and transportation infrastructure protection.

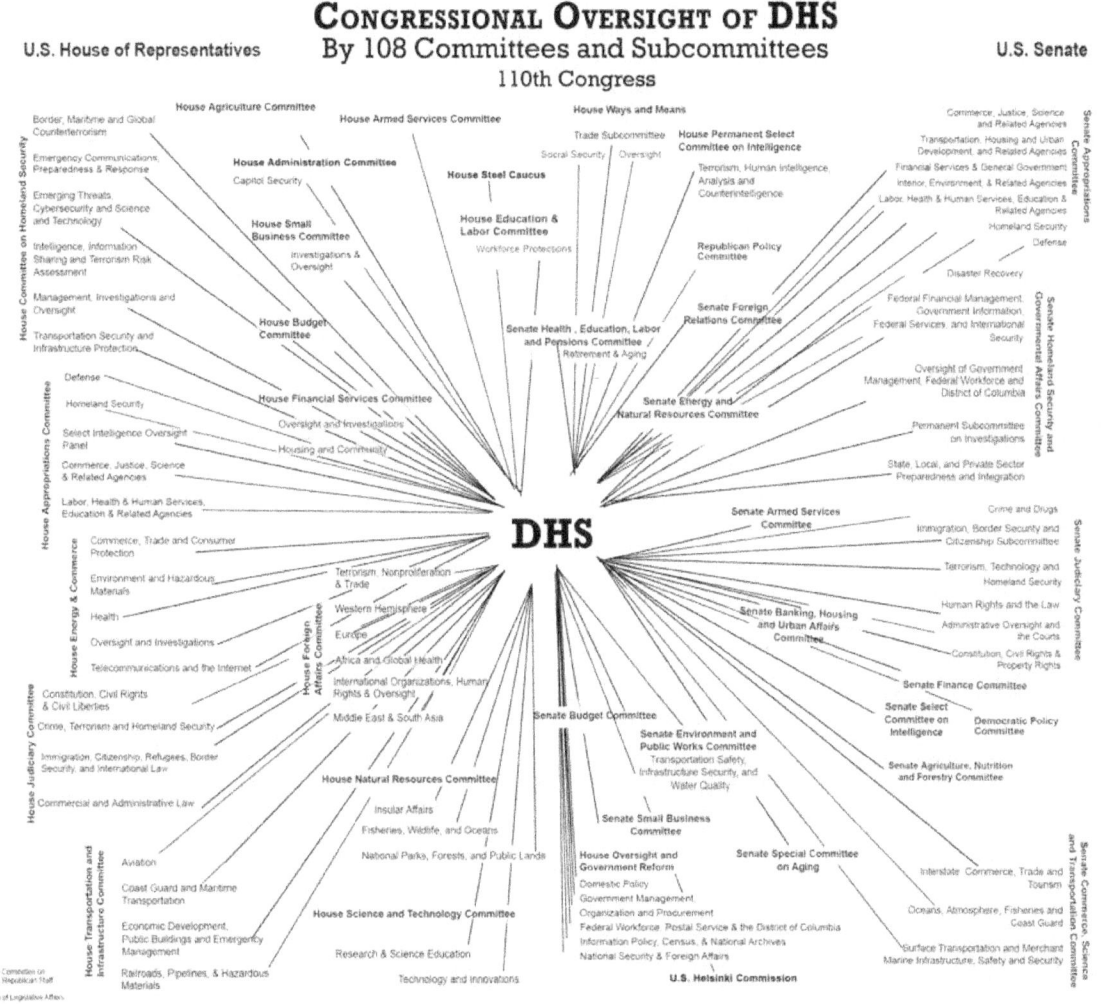